Toward a Wiser Colossus

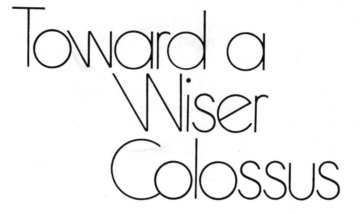

Reviewing and Recasting United States Foreign Policy

The Louis Martin Sears Lectures
Purdue University, 1970-71

Edited by James A. Stegenga

Purdue University Studies
Lafayette, Indiana
1972

Preface

THE LECTURES COLLECTED in this volume were made possible by a generous bequest from the late Louis Martin Sears, for thirty-six years a professor of history at Purdue University. Professor Sears probably revealed his motive forty-five years ago when he wrote:

> Foreign relations, then, constitute the highest challenge to the intelligence and good sense of the voter. The European autocrat of other days, called by heredity to the administration of affairs of state, made foreign affairs his first study, his abiding concern. His own greatness and the prosperity and existence of his country depended more upon a wise foreign policy than upon any other factor. The free citizen who has succeeded the autocrat in a world of which America is as much a part as Europe will prove false to his heritage if he displays an interest one whit less intelligent and continuous than that of his predecessor.

If it was appropriate for the citizen to be interested in foreign affairs forty-five years ago, it is critical for him to be interested, indeed involved, today when the stakes are so much greater and wisdom such a critical resource.

The lectures were given to large and enthusiastic audiences at Purdue University during the 1970-1971 academic year. Each author was later permitted to revise, extend, and update (to late 1971) his remarks for publication. And it was my enjoyable task to work with the authors on these revisions.

The six distinguished scholars and men of affairs are, of course, quite able to speak for themselves, and I would not presume to summarize their arguments. But they all touch on several important topics, and some common views emerge; perhaps it will help to identify several of these commonalities.

Each of these perceptive students of United States foreign policy is unhappy with America's recent performance on the international stage. Too much of the time the process has not

v

worked efficiently or, more importantly, wisely. Too many errors have been committed, too many opportunities missed. Two sources of our problems are frequently mentioned: first, the complexities of the situations to which our statesmen have to respond, and, second, the inadequacies of their responses. The situations are very complex largely because the United States has suddenly and only recently emerged as a superpower with far-flung interests precisely at the time when technology is stimulating sweeping changes world-wide. Perhaps understandably, our statesmen experience great difficulties reacting to such great challenges, to say nothing of mastering and thereby shaping their situations. And, at least several authors suggest, their difficulties are compounded by typically American romantic exuberance, naïve overconfidence, ideological fervor, a penchant for gimmickry, and a measure of immodesty, if not arrogance.

The suggestions these six experienced observers offer are based on their perceptive analyses of United States foreign policy in these challenging times; and they deserve our careful consideration.

J.A.S.

Contents

The Editor and the Authors

JAMES A. STEGENGA

is professor of political science, Purdue University. His books include *The Politics of Military Policy, The United Nations Force in Cyprus, Issues Before the 25th General Assembly,* and *The Global Community: A Brief Introduction to International Relations* (with W. Andrew Axline). Also an associate editor of *Society* magazine, he is presently completing an analysis of psychological explanations of warfare.

GEORGE W. BALL

has been involved in the formulation of United States policy since World War II when he served as associate general counsel of the Lend-Lease Administration and the Foreign Economic Administration and later as director of the United States Strategic Bombing Survey engaged in assessing the effect of Allied air operations on the German war economy. At the end of 1945, Mr. Ball resumed the practice of law and did not return to government service until January 1961 when President Kennedy appointed him under secretary of state for economic affairs. In December 1961, he became under secretary of state and held that post until his resignation in September 1966. From May 1968 until January 1969 he served as United States ambassador to the United Nations. Mr. Ball is presently a senior partner in the international investment banking firm of Lehman Brothers and is the author of *The Discipline of Power,* published in 1968.

THE RIGHT HONOURABLE DENIS HEALEY, MBE, MP,

was the British secretary of state for defense in the Wilson government from 1964 until 1970 and was named privy councillor at the time of his appointment. He is Labour member of

1

Parliament for the Yorkshire constituency of Leeds, East, and is now the official spokesman of the Labour Opposition on foreign policy and a member of the National Executive Committee of the Labour Party. From 1945 until 1952, Mr. Healey traveled widely, performing his duties as secretary of the Labour Party's International Department. Following his election to Parliament in 1952, he visited Moscow, the Middle and Far East, the Soviet Union, and the United States. As secretary of state for defence, he regularly attended meetings of the NATO Council, toured the Far East, and visited Washington. Mr. Healey is a member of the Royal Institute of International Affairs and the Institute of Strategic Studies. His publications include *Neutralism, NATO and American Security,* and *A Neutral Belt in Europe.*

ARNAUD de BORCHGRAVE

is *Newsweek* magazine's senior editor and has covered many of the major international news events and crises of our time. Since joining *Newsweek* in 1951, he has reported from over seventy countries and operates from headquarters in Paris with most of the world as his beat. De Borchgrave is certainly one of the most knowledgeable Middle-Eastern experts in the news media. One of his most notable feats of diplomatic journalism was successive interviews in 1969 with Egypt's President Nasser and Israel's Prime Minister Eshkol in which each national leader revealed many new terms for peace in the Near East. He conducted a similar exchange between President Sadat and Israel's Golda Meir in 1971. De Borchgrave was also the only correspondent to cover the original French air drop into Dienbienphu and he has covered the fighting in the Congo, the India-Pakistan war of 1965, and the Arab-Israeli war of 1967. He has had seven tours of duty in Vietnam, his last during the 1968 Tet offensive. He returned to Paris in time for the student riots and that summer went to Czechoslovakia to cover the Russian invasion.

IRVING LOUIS HOROWITZ

is professor of sociology at Rutgers University and chairman of its Livingston College division. Dr. Horowitz is editor-in-chief of *Society,* the largest social science magazine in the United States, and director of Studies in Comparative International Development at Rutgers. He has authored and edited many works, particularly in the field of Latin America and Third

World studies. Among his books are *The Rise and Fall of Project Camelot: Studies in the Relationship between Social Science and Political Practice, Three Worlds of Development: The Theory and Practice of International Stratification, Revolution in Brazil: Politics and Society in a Developing Nation, Masses in Latin America* and *Latin American Radicalism* which he edited with Josue de Castro and John Gerassi. Before joining the faculty at Rutgers, Dr. Horowitz was professor of sociology at Washington University for seven years and has also taught at Stanford University, the University of Wisconsin, the University of California, and, for several years, the University of Buenos Aires.

ALLEN S. WHITING

is professor of political science and an associate at the Center for Chinese Studies at the University of Michigan. He was deputy consul general in Hong Kong from 1966 until 1968 and had previously spent four years with the Department of State as director of the Office for Research and Analysis for the Far East. His official travels have taken him to India, Burma, Thailand, Laos, South Vietnam, Hong Kong, Taiwan, and Japan. After completing his Ph.D. at Columbia in 1952, Dr. Whiting was a Ford Foundation Fellow in Taiwan, Hong Kong, and Japan. In 1960 he served as a visiting associate professor at Columbia. He has authored three books, including *China Crosses the Yalu: The Decision to Enter the Korean War,* and has had numerous articles published in scholarly journals and popular publications. In 1969 he authored articles on China for both *Life* and *Look* and in 1971 joined *The New Republic* as a contributing editor. Dr. Whiting was among the experts invited to testify during the United States Senate hearings on the ABM program in 1969 and in 1971 testified before the Senate Foreign Relations Committee and the Joint Economic Committee on various aspects of United States policy toward China.

HANS J. MORGENTHAU

is Leonard Davis Distinguished Professor of Political Science at the City University of New York and Albert A. Michelson Distinguished Service Professor Emeritus of Political Science and Modern History at the University of Chicago. His view that the United States should be concerned primarily with its national interest rather than with world opinion has provoked consider-able controversy. Dr. Morgenthau was educated in Germany and received his doctorate in law summa cum laude from the University of Frankfurt. He practiced law in Germany and taught in Germany, Switzerland, and Spain before fleeing Nazism and settling in the United States in 1937. His most important books include *Scientific Man vs. Power Politics, Politics Among Nations, The Purpose of American Politics,* and *A New Foreign Policy for the United States.*

United States Foreign Relations:
Policy and Process
George W. Ball

CONTRARY TO THE MYTHOLOGY of the political scientists, the Department of State is not so much an institution as a figure of speech, a cathartic for Americans in an age of frustration. Blaming our troubles on the department is an established—perhaps even a necessary—form of national therapy—a treatment needed because now, more than ever, we live on a damned difficult and complicated planet. Since, in the words of T. S. Eliot, "Human kind cannot stand too much reality," some all-purpose scapegoat is obviously necessary and here is where the secretary of state and his department find their special métier; for the secretary exists, as Henry Adams long ago pointed out, "to deal with a world that Congress and the American people would rather ignore."

Not all the American people would ignore it perhaps, but certainly a fair percentage, of which the most conspicuous are columnists and editorial writers, would. Hobbled by the limitations of a stylized art form with a fixed limit of words, they are always in need of simple, forthright solutions to troublesome problems—so they invent them; and the fact that such oversimplified solutions are quite impracticable in the real world of foreign policy gives them a definite advantage over the Department of State. For the department—like any foreign office—cannot ignore the practical conditions under which relations with other nations must be shaped and carried out and it must seek to resolve all problems within the context of the nation's larger interests.

It is this latter necessity which leads to impatience and frustration. so that the merest mention of the department triggers a

5

string of abusive clichés. Because it must necessarily reject the easy answers, the department is condemned as "over-cautious," "bureaucratic," "obstructionist," "unimaginative," and much worse. (The litany of invective, though hackneyed, gains credence by repetition.) And every schoolboy knows what must be done with an institution that is thoroughly unsatisfactory: it must be reorganized.

Unhappily, such a naïve remedy makes very little sense, since it ignores the reality of the predicament—that there are no easy solutions for the intractable problems faced by a great power. Nevertheless, for many years, any number of boards, committees, and commissions, composed of serious, and often able, men and women, have solemnly gone about reshuffling the little boxes in the department's chart of organization, inventing new jobs or at least new titles, and preparing vast reports with numbered recommendations.

How much more useful if all that brain power had been focused on the substance of policy, searching for adequate means by which to test projected solutions or initiatives! Not quantifiable standards that ignore the all-important elements of will and purpose, but comprehensive, hard-nosed appraisals that leave no relevant considerations untouched. For, as we have—or should have—learned from Vietnam, it is all too easy to ignore the hard central questions: "Assuming that we command—or think we command—the resources to achieve a result beneficial to the interests of the United States in a limited area, what will be the total costs? And is the effort worth making if it harms the fabric of our foreign policy elsewhere in the world?"

In Vietnam the costs clearly outweighed any possible benefits. It is the textbook case to be studied with prayerful attention—a horrible example of where men of competence and good will became so preoccupied with the achievement of a narrow result in a limited area that they lost sight of the relation between cost and benefit. Impressed by the resources and ingenuity—and assuming the staying-power—of the American people, they put blind faith in what General DeGaulle used to call the "logic of number." Thus they concluded·quite mistakenly that a developed industrial country five thousand miles away could, by investing sufficient resources of men and material, determine the issue of a conflict between men of a different race that was at once an indigenous revolt and a foreign invasion; and—what is more— they assumed that it could, working from outside, construct a viable independent democratic state where none had ever existed before—provided only enough imagination and resources were deployed for the task. Influenced by faddish theories about "nation-building," they concluded that, with America's flair for what was called "social and political engineering," we could make bricks without the straw of a national tradition from clay that was historically friable and non-cohesive.

Yet, in spite of Vietnam, the vision of an America endowed with limitless capabilities is a myth that dies hard—and it still has its echoes in the banal demands of politicians and editorial writers who constantly call for "bold new initiatives," "new imaginative policies," and "fresh, affirmative approaches." Such phrases are the outward and visible signs of intellectual bank-ruptcy. When anybody speaks or writes such vacuous nonsense, he betrays a simple-minded assumption that there must exist for every problem a solution that the State Department could easily develop if it were really worth its salt—a solution he could cer-tainly work out himself if he did not have better things to do. For a hard-pressed scrivener, it is the coward's way out; with a paltry arsenal of ammunition, he will almost invariably save his last shots for the Department of State.

All this, of course, is not to suggest that condemnation of the department is limited to columnists—or, for that matter, to con-gressmen or bartenders or taxi drivers; invective also sounds with monotonous cacophony from college campuses, where a few omniscient professors long ago discovered that the bulk of our troubles derive from a doltish foreign service. It is a thought they nourish with enormous gusto, a patented mystical insight to explain all new disasters—and, like muezzins, their chants can be heard with clockwork regularity from the rarefied pinnacles of their ivory towers.

I

Though predictable in their reflexes, those experts are far from original; consciously or not, they are aping an ancient tra-dition. Like the United States, Rome held diplomacy in low repute. So long as she could enforce her will by the phalanx she did not need to parley, and it was only with the attrition of physical power in the latter days of the empire that cunning came to command a high premium. Then adroit Byzantine diplomats kept the enemy off balance by setting one barbarian tribe against another and buying the friendship of frontier tribes. As unprincipled as they were skillful, they wielded the Christian faith as an instrument of aggrandizement—something to be imposed through conquest or corruption.

Since tactics of bargaining and maneuver practiced with such high sophistication are obnoxious to less complicated peoples, it is hardly surprising that Byzantine diplomacy became more an epithet than a historical reference. Yet if, as the learned Prussian general claimed, war really is the extension of diplomacy by other means, diplomacy, even of the Byzantine variety, was still considerably more humane than war. But who cares? Mankind, perpetually in search of simplification, has regularly preferred the warrior to the schemer.

Shrewd as were the Byzantine emperors who advanced the diplomatic arts during the latter days of Rome, it was the medieval Italians who carried on from there. Unlimited maneuvering was possible in the Italian city-states, which, driven by fierce rivalries and with no loyalty to one another, invented endless combinations and permutations of cabal, conspiracy, and alliance. It was here, during the thirteenth and fourteenth centuries, that adroit and unscrupulous virtuosos evolved the forms and practices of modern diplomacy.

Yet, though they added a flamboyant flair to Byzantine methods, they still did not give the profession a good name. Not only is the arbitrament of force more understandable than cleverness or shrewdness, but also most men view these latter qualities with suspicion and deplore them on moral grounds.

II

All of this played a part in shaping the American psyche since, in the credo of the Founding Fathers, the Old World was a sink of corruption with diplomacy high among the venal sins of commission. Nor were diplomatic practices compatible with the egalitarian posture of the new America—the "city high on the hill"—the evangelical archetype of the New World.

Yet even though diplomats were odious relics of the system that we Americans were putting behind us, the Yankee trader still had more than a trace of Byzantium in his character. No matter how pious he might appear, he could usually hold his own with the devious dukes and mendacious barons of the Old World. Consider, for example, Benjamin Franklin, the canniest and most realistic of the Founding Fathers, who did not let principle prevent him from concluding a peace behind the backs of our French and Spanish allies, later justifying his action on the high moral ground that we were about to be double-crossed ourselves.

In broad terms, American diplomats in our earlier history fell into two categories. The first were politicians. Some were able men; others were commissioned only because they were unemployed or inconvenient to have around. As a group, they wore their democracy with flamboyance and often as a chip on the shoulder, delighting to scandalize the chancelleries of Europe, as, for example, when Buchanan bravely stood against the wearing of court dress at the Court of St. James. (He finally settled for a black coat, then added a sword so as not to be mistaken for a waiter.) That was good fun in an otherwise humorless profession. Usually it did America no harm, though sometimes our politician diplomats created vexing problems. A New Orleans political hack named Pierre Soule, sent on a mission to Spain in 1754, indulged in endless slapstick, one or two duels and finally connived to produce the absurd Ostend Manifesto, an unauthorized statement by our envoys to Europe denouncing Spain for refusing to sell us Cuba.

Apart from the politicians was a serious second group. Typified by John Quincy Adams, they were, in the elevated vernacular of present-day politics, "effete Eastern snobs." Not only were they well educated but, of necessity, financially well off, since diplomacy had little room for the poor but well-trained professional. Until late in the nineteenth century, for example, England made it an explicit qualification of its foreign service that a candidate must establish his ability to support himself, a requirement that was frequently an understatement, since one of the recognized instruments of diplomacy in many posts—particularly St. Petersburg—was the bribing of courtiers, so that even the richest ambassadors often returned home with fortunes disastrously depleted.

III

For obvious reasons a diplomacy shaped by dynastic manipulations was difficult to adapt to a democracy, which is why we Americans inherited not only traditions but neuroses. Even after a century and a half of experience, we have scarcely stopped thinking of ourselves as a brash young democratic nation with a mission to transform the world by our own virtuous example. Certainly we are far from fully adjusted to the diplomatic necessities of a superpower compelled to play a dominant world role.

Twenty years ago we faced a problem that baffled many Americans. Emerging from the Second World War as the most powerful nation in history, we discovered with shock and dismay that, with the advent of nuclear weapons, the two wide oceans we regarded as our defensive moat no longer insulated our homes and factories against enemy attack. Overnight, we confronted a paradox too baffling for easy comprehension: how to reconcile unprecedented power with unprecedented vulnerability. Since it was a puzzle quite beyond our own experience, we reacted, as people have so often reacted to unfathomable danger, by explaining the inexplicable in the cheap but facile terms of betrayal. We sought scapegoats; and what better targets could be found than our diplomats and the institution they served?

Occupationally detached from our national life and set apart from the rest of us, our diplomats were sitting ducks for the *francs tireurs*. Since they spoke foreign tongues and made their living consorting with foreigners, how could anyone possibly expect them to be 100 percent American?

It was a situation tailor-made for a loud-mouthed demagogue from Wisconsin and, in the absence of a firm presidential rebuke, he made the most of it. In the ensuing dark night of anger, suspicion, and abuse, our foreign service was reduced to a glutinous mass, suffering not only from injustice and obloquy but losing both the confidence of the people and confidence in themselves. It was an interlude of manipulated confusion, compounded by the fact that most Americans have never understood what their foreign office does, how it operates, or what it contributes to our strength and security. It is time we learned.

IV

A foreign office is, in lawyer's language, *sui generis;* it is like no other institution, normally playing a mute and inarticulate role in carrying out policies made at a higher level by whoever happens to be the president or secretary of state. It is not well placed to win kudos. Such foreign policy triumphs as may be achieved will be claimed by the president then in power, while—like any professional service—the department is expected to hold the bag for failure.

The first point to learn about a foreign office is that it is not a factory. It does not manufacture or package or sell a shining product called a foreign policy decision. Nor can its performance be improved by repositioning a production line in order to improve what is incessantly referred to in a singularly fatuous phrase as the "decision-making process." In fact, obsessive emphasis on elaborate machinery is the best way I can think of to stultify innovation and impair effective policy.

But if a foreign office is not a factory, what is it? To answer that question, let us briefly look at our own diplomatic establishment, at the center of which is the Department of State and its missions around the world. Let us start with those missions which in almost all cases we now call embassies.

Before the Second World War, our missions in smaller countries were referred to as legations and headed by ministers. But with the proliferation of new small countries and the egalitarianism expressed in the United Nations Charter, President Roosevelt began a process of relabelling. By 1950 almost the only legations left were in Budapest and Sophia, and today, outside the Iron Curtain countries, we have an embassy in every country with which we have diplomatic relations.

The reason for this development is not hard to identify. New countries, dazzled by suddenly achieving a place in the sun, are status conscious. They want the de luxe treatment, or, in other words, the dignity that comes from having an American ambassador resident in their country. At the same time, they take pride

in being able to send an ambassador to Washington (and sometimes duplicate him at frightful expense by maintaining a second
ambassador at the United Nations in New York).

Quite naturally, our senior career diplomats are not happy
with the practice, since what is upgrading for new countries
debases the ambassadorial title. It is not that the club of
ambassadors has grown so large (the United States now has
about 120, including those who hold personal rank but are not
accredited to any country) but, as someone said of the British
Commonwealth, what was once Boodles becomes the R.A.C.
when our envoys to Ougadougo and London are both members.*
Yet, though the top of the service may complain, the new practice gladdens the hearts of the younger foreign service officers,
as well as of those older officers who could never aspire to a
Class I post. Moreover, having so many ambassadorial appoint-
ments available is an important boon to presidents because it
enables them to pay off a lavish but incompetent campaign
contributor without inciting a major country to declare war.

V

So we now have 117 embassies on all the continents of the
world. What do they do?

First, they collect information of all kinds—political, economic
and even cultural—and send it to Washington, in most cases on a
daily basis. Included among the most important telegrams are
the ambassador's appraisal of the current situation and prospects
for the future, as well as his recommendations regarding the
course of action we should pursue in dealing with a particular
emerging situation.

Obviously, the usefulness of such recommendations depends on
the competence of the ambassador. If our man in Moscow or
Prague or Paris is a seasoned diplomat of recognized judgment,
his advice will be given careful attention even at the highest
levels; if he is a political hack or even a professional noted for
certain biases, the department will know what junior drafted the

---

* Boodles is an exclusive London sporting club, whereas anyone with an
automobile and the minimal membership fee may join the R.A.C. (the
Royal Automobile Club), an organization roughly akin to the American
Automobile Association (AAA). (*Editor's note.*)

dispatch or how to discount the biases. Other factors also enter into the assessment. In cases where an ambassador remains too long in a particular post, he may tend to become an apologist for the country to which he is posted, or even a defender of the particular government with which he does his daily business no matter how corrupt or repressive it may be. He develops, in the language of the trade, a pernicious disease known as "localitis," which means he is ready for reassignment. Even that may not cure him, if he is the kind of man or woman who mistakes an ambassadorial post for a good-will mission. Thus, whenever I hear it said that Jenkins, our envoy to Graustark, is a "wonderful ambassador, the most popular man in the country, everybody loves him," then I know old Jenkins has had it. He should be got out of there just as rapidly as possible before he gives away his ambassadorial flag.

When an embassy telegram reaches Washington, it is routed for action to the appropriate country desk officer in the appropriate regional bureau, while information copies are sent to a great number of other officers in the department and in other agencies and departments all over Washington.

It is the five regional bureaus—for European affairs, for Near Eastern and South Asian affairs, for Inter-American affairs, for East Asian and Pacific affairs, and for African affairs—that have the prime responsibility for the day-to-day conduct of our foreign policy; they are the beating heart of the foreign office organism. They are assisted with technical help and advice by ten functional bureaus that concentrate on such matters as economics, congressional relations, press relations, educational and cultural affairs, and so on.

It is the function of each regional bureau (and specifically of the assistant secretary of state who heads that bureau) to give day-to-day instructions to the ambassadors in all embassies within its regional jurisdiction, as well as to handle relations with the ambassadors that the governments in the region have sent to Washington. Thus, the assistant secretary of a regional bureau has direct and immediate responsibility for the development and guidance of our foreign policy within his geographical area. Obviously, his radius of vision is broader than that of our ambassador in any particular country post. But, though he must appraise the advice of the ambassador in the context of all that is happening in a whole region, that still does not mean that he has the final word on other than fairly routine matters.

Problems that may affect our relations with other areas are discussed with the appropriate assistant secretary for each area affected; if an agreement cannot be reached on the course to follow, or if a situation is particularly sticky or may require a reconsideration of existing policies or some new American response or initiative, it is reviewed with either the secretary or under secretary, who have co-extensive responsibilities that are world-wide. Sometimes this is done by an assistant secretary on his own motion; sometimes a summons is issued by the secretary or under secretary who have also read the most important telegrams. If the problem is primarily economic and the department happens at the time to have an under secretary for economic affairs, he is the one consulted—at least in the first instance.

It is at this point that policies are seen in their broadest implications, since it is for the secretary or under secretary to make sure that, though a policy pursued in Africa might seem to serve us well in that continent, it does not create problems in our relations with some Middle Eastern or Asian country, or even with one or more of our Western European allies. In other words, it is the function of the top command of the State Department to see United States policy as a coherent whole and to give it direction that takes into account our long-term as well as short-term objectives.

VI

Quite frequently, of course, important matters arise which cannot be dealt with by even the secretary of state and must be handled by the president himself. It is with respect to such matters that a great deal of nonsense has been spoken and written, since many have been so bedazzled by the mechanistic beauty of the so-called "decision-making process" that, wittingly or unwittingly, they have created a totally false impression of where and how a president gets the advice that he factors into his decisions.

As one might expect, there is no rigid pattern. It varies from administration to administration, primarily depending on the temperament and background of the president and his relation ship with, and attitude toward, his secretary of state. At one end of the spectrum was the situation under President Truman, who had, in my view, almost ideal relations with Dean Acheson, his secretary of state. Having no exaggerated faith in his own foreign policy genius, he left to the secretary the central direction of our foreign policy, while backing him to the utmost in the decisions he made.

Again in the Eisenhower administration the secretary of state, John Foster Dulles, was left with substantially a free hand. Mr. Dulles was, in President Eisenhower's appraisal—which was by no means universally shared—"the greatest secretary of state in American history."

But though Mr. Acheson and Mr. Dulles each had the confidence of his president and was thus left a large area of discretion, the two secretaries differed substantially in their attitudes toward the State Department. This was reflected in the degree to which the department was involved and how well the talents of the department were utilized during the two periods.

Every secretary of state has, or should have, two major roles: to be at once the president's principal advisor on foreign policy and the head of the whole foreign policy apparatus of the government—or what Dean Acheson has called the president's "executive agent." Mr. Dulles was almost exclusively interested in the first role; he had relatively little interest in the Department of State. In fact, he betrayed such lack of trust in his own colleagues that he even considered, when first appointed, separating himself physically from the department and establishing his office in the Executive Office Building near the president. Mr. Acheson, who was fully at home with the department, preferred to remain close to the troops.

It was while Mr. Acheson was secretary of state that the National Security Council was created with a small staff. It was the function of that staff, presided over by an executive secretary, to gather together papers flowing into the White House primarily from the State and Defense Departments and the intelligence community, and so organize them that they could be presented to the president in an orderly fashion. At the same time, the council was to bring its particular inputs of specialized advice to bear on relevant questions.

During President Truman's administration, the council operated in an inconspicuous manner; its staff was spare and anonymous, consisting of only professional officers, and its function was largely mechanical. But during the administration of President Eisenhower and reflecting his military habits, the council was used as the underpinning for a superstructure of boards and committees that enormously increased the output of planning documents, as well as statements of policy.

Unhappily, what these boards and committees did was to create the impression of orderliness without contributing to the orderly process by which decisions are made. They were devoted not to challenging existing preconceptions systematically but codifying orthodoxy and, by their very existence, they came between the president and his principal advisors, the heads of the key departments.

One of the first acts of President Kennedy was to sweep away this formalistic structure, while at the same time transforming the role of the executive secretary of the National Security Council into the president's advisor for national security affairs, or, as the newspapers have shortened it, his national security advisor. Since this was not long after the McCarthy period and the State Department was then in a depleted state of morale and effectiveness, the quickest method of injecting new energy and ideas into our foreign policy was to develop a staff of experts in the White House itself to act as a miniature and competitive Department of State with personnel assigned to monitor each regional bureau.

This staff, initially gathered together in the early days of 1961, consisted largely of young activists from university faculties, together with a handful of particularly able young foreign service officers. It contained among its members what one of them later described as "a new brand of academic social scientists who had studied counter-guerrilla warfare and were anxious to put their theories to the test."

In competition with such rapidly-moving adversaries, the demoralized and overgrown State Department—accustomed to a slower tempo—was no more effective than the Spanish Armada against Drake's highly maneuverable ships, while the frenetic young men on the White House staff made no effort to conceal their contempt for the career service.

This development could have completely demoralized the department if the man in charge at the White House, McGeorge Bundy, had not recognized the problem and taken a strong hand to keep his energetic minions in line. Even so, there was such confusion at the beginning of the administration that, before Mr. Bundy got things fully under control, the secretary's authority, even over his own department, was in jeopardy.

Junior foreign service officers, lost in the middle reaches of the department, were initially startled, then flattered, when they received telephone calls from the president himself. (It gave them something to dine out on for weeks, though at least one of them suffered agonies of apprehension when he responded profanely on the assumption that his leg was being pulled.) Yet, when unknown young men began in the name of "the White House" to request memoranda and reports from State Department officers who complied without approval of their superiors, it was clearly time to call a halt, since that way lay chaos. Fortunately, Mr. Bundy was fully sensitive to the untidiness that threatened and imposed sensible procedures. Still it was some time before the career officers of the department learned not to react blindly at the mention of the magic words "White House," but to find out who at the White House really wanted a memorandum prepared or study made, since it might merely be some curious and pragmatic young man, fresh from an ivy-encrusted scholar's cell, who was working the levers at random to find out what would happen.

VII

Not that the building of competing State Departments was confined to the White House. Because, under policies followed throughout the last two decades, our military have had the mission of maintaining a cordon around that whole area of the Eurasian land mass under Communist control, the Defense Department has been necessarily concerned with programs of military assistance, arms sales, foreign bases agreements, and crisis planning involving all outposts of the globe. Responding to a natural bureaucratic instinct, it has built within the Office of Secretary of Defense a miniature foreign office, organized in the best tradition of regional lines, called the Office of the Assistant Secretary of Defense for International Security Affairs (or ISA). In addition to the more than 320 personnel employed in ISA, the roster of the Organization of the Joint Chiefs numbers over two thousand, of whom only 900 are military officers.

Though these staffs are obviously overblown and redundant in function with the department (it is necessary for the State Department to maintain a special Bureau of Political-Military Affairs with a staff of ninety just for liaison with Defense), they have not seriously interfered with the work of the department. No doubt this has been in large part due to the fact that the ISA was, during the years of my last tour in the bureaucracy, under the direction first of William Bundy and then of the late John McNaughton—both eminently sensible and sophisticated men.

In effect, the Defense Department's intrusions into foreign policy were of minor importance when compared with those of the White House staff. But even the activities of the White House staff created no serious problems for the State Department during the 1960s; they served more as a goad and pace-setter. Unquestionably, the ebullient young recruits to McGeorge Bundy's staff were far more fertile in bright new thoughts than the shell-shocked officers in the Department of State, and I can understand why any president, wishing to bring about quick change and fast movement in our foreign policy, would have been tempted to build up his White House resources. Still it was an improvisation required by a special set of circumstances, which did not offer a desirable long-term solution. That could be achieved only by improving the quality of output of the department.

This process was already partly under way when President Kennedy was assassinated. Several of the members of Mr. Bundy's staff had been transferred to the department, and I think it likely that more might have followed. Some quickly adjusted to the practices of the department where they learned to make their energies and ideas felt; at least one, however, proved an utter disaster. Brilliant, articulate, but headstrong and impulsive, he could not bring himself to work within a disciplined institution, side by side with men of more experience if perhaps less imagination, and he left for greener pastures.

I mention this in making a point too often neglected—that even though the department may have seemed overly negative and unreceptive to new ideas, it was frequently right. I do not go so far as a French brandy distiller I once knew who contended that "any new idea is a bad idea"; yet an idea is not good just because it has not been tried before—or even been tried before and failed. Many of the men who came to work in the White House added to the content and color of what began to take shape as the Kennedy foreign policy. But, being apart from the mainstream of action, they did not have to defend their ideas against officers in other bureaus attuned to possible repercussions elsewhere in the world; nor were they required to take responsibility for carrying out what they proposed or defend it before the Congress. Thus, there was occasionally a tendency to drive forward without taking full account of all the ruts, roadblocks, and dangerous curves ahead, which sometimes resulted in a distortion in emphasis, if not an error in substance, that might otherwise have been avoided.

The gravest danger in the improvised White House staff of the early 1960s was, as I have suggested, its precedental value—the possibility that it might start a trend which could, over the years ahead, culminate in the creation of a second State Department in the White House that could seriously clutter up the development and administration of a coherent foreign policy. No one who has been exposed to the bureaucracy needs Professor Parkinson to point out that every organization is inherently expansionist; and one has only to note the fact that Dr. Kissinger's staff today numbers more than 130 (more than three times the size of the Bundy staff) to realize that this trend is already well along.

Perhaps the buildup of such an eager band of experts is the only way to attract able talent to our foreign policy establishment, though the evidence is mostly the other way. Members of the White House staff emit a special luminosity, but I would be sad if I thought that young academics seriously interested in foreign policy would make glamor a condition to service. It is possible some may feel that the State Department, as presently constituted, cannot offer the scope for their talents commensurate with their own high appraisal; but if that is their view, I would suggest they stay home anyway. If they wish to be involved only in high level decisions after the hard work has been done, they can only be a dangerous nuisance. Theoreticians without responsibility, experience, or humility should be locked up in their ivory towers for the good of the state.

VIII

Where the White House staff has so far had the advantage is not merely in its ability to recruit but to merchandise its own ideas, since, on the whole, the members of the staff are professionally articulate, while the department is notoriously tongue-tied.

I stress this point because it accounts for a great deal of the difficulty the Department of State has experienced in responding adequately to the requirements of our recent presidents, as well as defending itself against charges of inadequacy. I found many unexpected pools of mute talent in the department—foreign service officers or groups of officers who had ideas and imagination, yet were incapable of expressing those ideas in straightforward and persuasive argument. In fact, too many members of the foreign service seem proficient in every language except English.

During my tenure in the department I tried without much success to improve the quality of expression. I told the Foreign Service Association that I had always thought the simple declarative sentence was one of the noblest architectural works of man but that I had found little agreement with that proposition in the department. And I am sure that I irritated many of my colleagues by bucking letters and memoranda back to their authors with the note, "Please send this to the translation department and have it put into English."

Without doubt, the written output of the department is lamentable; scrutinizing the answers to the most important congressional mail that, as under secretary, I was supposed to sign each morning, I sometimes wondered why the congressional view of the department was as charitable as it was. Quite frankly, I have never seen such fatuous clichés, unresponsive answers, and club-footed evasions as those assembled (after twenty-four clearances) in the normal State Department answer to a congressional inquiry. I used to think we could have done better with a computer; at least it would not have felt self-satisfied with the result.

Just why this deterioration in departmental prose has occurred I do not know since, after all, diplomacy has an honorable literary tradition. In years past ambassadors took pride in the elegance and sprightliness of their weekly or monthly despatches, and the practice of turning out lucidly—and often vividly—written minutes and telegrams still survives in the British Foreign Office. Even in the United States such a tradition is not wholly unknown. Some of our older diplomats, such as, for example, George Kennan, who is a professional, and David Bruce, who might as well be, are distinguished writers, and their telegrams were always a delight to read.

It is possible, of course, that technology—on which we blame most of our troubles these days—can be held responsible for the degradation of diplomatic prose. Cables are a limited art form and the telephone is a corrupting instrument conducive to the kind of communication known as "stream of consciousness" —or all too often, "trickle of consciousness."

Yet, whatever the effect of technology on messages between the department and its overseas missions, that alone cannot explain the spate of turgid and cliché-ridden letters and memoranda produced in Washington. Certainly this was one of the department's inadequacies that most irritated the bright young men in the White House—and with reason. It put the department at a distinct disadvantage in the presentation of its own ideas to the president, and quite incapable of providing sparkling paragraphs for the president's own public statements on foreign policy.

IX

The most serious danger that may result from developing a burgeoning staff in the White House that threatens in time to become a second foreign office is not overlapping and duplication, but the potential dilution of the authority of the secretary of state and the interposition between him and the president of a second executive agent. That is what Dean Acheson had in mind when he said he would be unwilling to serve as secretary of state under the present conditions of the job.

Unhappily, in trying to solve this problem, a banal accident of geography interferes. Today the office of the secretary of state is in a section of Washington quaintly known as Foggy Bottom, in a glass and stone structure a quarter mile away from the president, while the president's assistant for national security affairs is at his elbow. It is an elemental fact that any executive—including any president—is most likely to be influenced by a man physically close at hand who can be in his office on three seconds' notice. This tendency is intensified when that man is free from all the routine burdens and responsibilities, both administrative and protocolaire, of the secretary, is immune from congressional appearances and contacts which take up a great deal of the secretary's time, and—because he is on the president's own staff—is attuned to the nuances of the prevailing palace atmosphere. A wise man once said that "nothing propinks like propinquity," and that aphorism has definite relevance to the relationship we are considering.

Historically, the State Department inhabited the rococo edifice next door to the White House now called the Executive Office Building, and I think it might be a good idea for the vital nucleus of the department—the secretary and under secretary together with the geographic bureaus—to move back again. That depends, of course, on the interests and inclinations of each particular president, but if a president intends to spend a good deal of his time on foreign policy, he would do well to have his secretary of state close at hand.

This point is not in clear relief by the situation now prevailing. The present national security advisor, Dr. Henry Kissinger, is an exceptionally brilliant and articulate man who has spent his entire adult life thinking and writing about foreign policy, while the present secretary, William Rogers—though a man of quality, experienced in the law and in government—was coopted from private life without much prior exposure to the field. As a result, not only does Dr. Kissinger's voice now ring through loud and clear, but many of the most able career officers have come to feel that neither they nor the State Department are playing much more than a mechanical role in the formulation and execution of policy.

Such a situation is obviously not healthy but, what is even more serious, it confirms a trend that could create major problems in the future. It tends to make the State Department a dispirited place, as it is today at most levels, which is scarcely the way to inspire either hard work or adventurous thinking. Yet governments are not run for the benefit of their institutions—quite the other way around—and the fact that leading elements in the foreign service may be crying in their beer is not in itself a major disaster.

What is important is that, without the orderly participation of the department in transmitting ideas and analysis through the secretary to the president, the president is denied that testing of views against the accumulated experience of the department that may save us from ill-advised moves in time of crisis.

X

Paradoxically, in writing about President Nixon, who tends to make his decisions alone or after consultation with only one or two top advisors, press reports have tended to create the impression that the processes by which foreign policy is made are now more elaborate and institutionalized than ever. In other words, at a time when the established departments of government—at least in the field of foreign policy, and I suspect in other fields as well—have less of a role than in previous administrations, a great deal of newsprint has been devoted to describing the new maze of committees and subcommittees set up under the National Security Council to help make policy.

All of this sounds a good deal like a revival of the super-structure of committees, including the Operations Coordination Board, that flowered in President Eisenhower's day and were rooted out by President Kennedy. Yet—given the contrast in personalities and working habits between Mr. Nixon and General Eisenhower and between Mr. Rogers and Mr. Dulles—I cannot believe that they operate in anything like the same way. General Eisenhower liked institutionalized decisions with unanimous recommendations—they were in harmony with his background of military practice—but they would appear not in accord with the training of Mr. Nixon, whose background is the law and not soldiering.

Thus, when the newspapers create the impression that decisions taken by the president reflect the views expressed at solemn proceedings of the National Security Council, they are playing games with their readers.

For most Americans, far better acquainted with the ways of business than of government, mention of the National Security Council evokes visions of a board of directors—an analogy completely misleading. A corporation's board of directors can fire the company's president; the president of the United States can fire all the members of the National Security Council except the vice president. Neither the United States cabinet nor the National Security Council has any power whatever. The sensible question for any president is whether those particular members of his government who happen to be designated by statute as members of his National Security Council are the men he wants to consult with seriously on a particular foreign policy issue.

Certainly, neither Presidents Kennedy nor Johnson, under whom I served, ever used the National Security Council as an instrument for making major decisions, and for quite good reasons. The statutory members of the council are the president, the vice president, the secretaries of state and defense, and the head of the Office of Emergency Management (now called the Office of Emergency Preparedness).

Lamentable as some may find it, it is not the practice of presidents to use their vice presidents as serious foreign policy advisors. (Whatever the fundamental reasons for this, they are known, if at all, only to psychologists and professional politicians.) Nor is any president likely to wish even to discuss foreign policy moves in the presence of the head of the Office of Emergency Preparedness, a minor functionary whose principal duties are to coordinate federal disaster relief to the states and oversee strategic stockpiles.

Thus, the only two statutory members of the council whose advice the president would, in any event, certainly seek, are the secretaries of state and defense—and, since he is in touch with them constantly, formal NSC meetings are quite unnecessary.

As is the case with all committees, the National Security Council has been the victim of a creeping hypertrophy, with the practice developing for an increasing number of officials to attend meetings. Thus, while under secretary of state, I was regularly invited to NSC meetings, along with the head of the CIA, and so frequently were the secretary of the treasury, the chairman of the Joint Chiefs of Staff, always the national security advisor, and from time to time, additional officials, as events required.

Both Presidents Kennedy and Johnson were quite aware that the National Security Council was more a formal than a functioning institution, and when President Kennedy was faced with the appallingly dangerous problem of the Cuban missile crisis in October 1962, he set up a purely *ad hoc* group called the Executive Committee (or, as the press later called it, "ExCom"), some of the members of which normally sat with the NSC, and some which did not. It was taken for granted that ExCom was somehow attached to the NSC, but nobody thought to ask just how, since certainly at least one statutory member of the council never knew about the missile crisis until he heard the president's television speech after ExCom had been battling the problem for a week.

Thus, when Presidents Kennedy and Johnson held formal meetings of the NSC, it was not with the thought that those meetings would contribute to the making of other than quite minor decisions. When major decisions were to be made, each president consulted discreetly and selectively with those individuals whom he deemed best informed and whose judgment he most valued on the specific issue; then, having more often than not already made up his mind, he called a meeting of the National Security Council to inform the other members of his government, give them the feeling that they had had their day in court, and make sure that they accepted the decision and would close ranks once they knew it had been made.

This is, in my view, the only way a formally prescribed instrument such as the National Security Council can be intelligently used and I·am certain that, in this regard, Mr. Nixon follows the same practice as his predecessors. That this is, in fact, the case finds support in the way he is said to have made the important decision to go into Cambodia. According to the *New York Times* of May 10, 1970, President Nixon assigned the task of devising alternative approaches to what is called the Washington Special Action Group, but, according to the *Times,* their responsibility was only "to prepare various contingency plans and assess possible reaction to them from the Soviet Union, Communist China and Hanoi." That was a purely technical task; it was designed merely to furnish raw material on which a decision might be made. The actual decision was made by the president alone two nights later and announced to Secretary of State Rogers and Secretary of Defense Melvin Laird the next morning. Thus, concludes the *New York Times*, "The careful decision-making process of the National Security Council . . . was largely bypassed."

I do not make this comment critically because, though I have serious reservations as to the rightness of the decision, I think that, in making it, the president followed the flexible procedure that presidents have regularly used. What is important to realize —but what many still forget—is that we do not have a collective executive, and—except for the vice president—the members of the NSC are merely officials who serve at the pleasure of the president, some or all of whom he may or may not wish to consult on a particular question. The NSC as a body has no permanently delegated authority to decide anything, and no additional dignity is given to a decision by the fact that it has been run past the NSC. All that counts is what the president himself decides, and if he wishes to use the NSC as a formal mechanism for recording his decisions or transmitting them to the balance of the government, that is up to him; he could accomplish the same thing by a personal memorandum.

Over twenty years ago a task force report on foreign affairs organization prepared for the Hoover Commission expressed concern at the possible expansion of jurisdiction of the National Security Council, which had then been in existence less than two years, lamenting that the council seemed to have terms of reference "so broad that in the name of security it can and does get into numerous matters of foreign affairs which are strictly not its business." In the light of all we have since learned, this comment would seem to have missed the point. The real danger stemming from the council is not that the president may take its deliberations too seriously; it is rather that such a large staff may be constructed under the NSC umbrella as to interpose a serious barrier between the president and his secretary of state who presides over a department comprising the foreign affairs machinery of the United States—a department of wide experience that must be brought into close relationship with the executive authority of the president if decisions are to take into account the full range and emphasis of our interests around the world.

To try to build up a super State Department within the White House would, thus, be an evasion of the basic problem. The proper thrust of effort for any administration should be to see to it that the State Department is not superseded, but rather is improved in tone and quality and brought even more completely into the formulation and execution of policy. The last thing I would favor is the creation of any intermediate layer of officialdom between the president and his principal cabinet members, and I can think of nothing more mischievous than for the United States to adopt the parting recommendation of President Eisenhower for a first secretary of the government, to oversee all foreign affairs agencies.

XI

In insisting on the primacy of the secretary of state's advice on foreign policy, I am not suggesting that the Department of State is perfect, or that it could not be improved by some tinkering with its structure. Like all human institutions, it is fallible, and the department has had more than its share of vicissitudes. There is no doubt that the dark days of the McCarthy era left their mark on a whole generation of foreign service officers and wrought damage to the spirit and prestige of the department, from which it has not yet fully recovered. It drove many out of the diplomatic service in despair that Secretary of State Dulles not only showed little interest in defending his own organization but dealt the department a brutal blow when he acquiesced in the installation of McCarthy's own minion, Scott McLeod, to rule over the department's internal security. (Mr. McLeod, let me add parenthetically, is best remembered for the Elbert Hubbard homily displayed on his desk: "An ounce of loyalty is worth a pound of brains.") Not only did such action and inaction drive away good men or reduce them to cautious ineffectiveness, but it seriously impeded the recruitment of new blood. Finally, it definitely put a damper on bright ideas and encouraged a low-risk policy under which the pedestrian became the norm. As a result, in the words of one victim of this period, "Many cautious mediocrities rose to the top."

Clearly we have come a long way from that lamentable period, and the department is now staffed with men and women of reasonable competence. This does not mean, however, that a great deal more should not be done to improve its spirit and capability.

Today efforts are being made to rejuvenate the department, and to encourage the generation of fresh thought. Some are well conceived, others leave much to be desired.

Not long ago I was visited by a representative of the department equipped with pencil and notepad who wished to interview me as part of the work in preparation of a report of a "Task Force on the Stimulation of Creativity," which had been established in the department. This, I confess, momentarily put me off, since I had never thought of using a committee in connection with creativity; the two seemed antithetical. But since I was asked the direct question of what I would recommend, I replied to my inquisitor that the best way I could think of to stimulate creativity would be to fire all the uninspired minds in the department and hire creative ones, since I doubted the objective could be achieved by gimmicks.

I recognize, of course, that no matter how attractive my proposal might appear to an incoming secretary of state, it is the one proposal most difficult of execution. Given the protection accorded to status under both civil and foreign service regulations, there is probably no way to get rid of deadwood fast enough to free the upper levels for the rapid advancement of bright young men and women.

Like all professional services, the Foreign Service is largely self-managing, and it is beset with its own share of vested interests and rigidities. As a small, elite corps (there are only about three thousand foreign service officers), the principle of mutual protection—or perhaps more accurately reciprocal protection—operates with considerable effectiveness, and this necessarily involves the usual quantum of internal politics. Among other rigidities is the insistence that young officers endure a boring apprenticeship during their early years which, all too often, means stamping passports in some consular office in a remote and unimportant country with disastrous cuisine and a bad climate. When I was in the department I made an effort to get this practice stopped, since it seemed to me that the best recruiting officer for the service was the most recent entrant; it was his reports to the college campus he had only recently left that would carry the most conviction with graduates just facing a career decision. Nonetheless, senior members of the service strenuously objected to any change in the practice. After all, they had been through just such a period of dull grubbing and look what it had done for them! Thus, they insisted, every new entrant to the service should be made to go through the same apprenticeship.

I am encouraged by the fact that in 1967 a group of young turks in the service energetically went about getting control of the Foreign Service machinery. They have made their influence felt and no doubt some useful reforms will emerge from the effort—though it is too early to say just how much of a permanent mark they will leave.

XII

I have complained of the literary deficiencies of the Foreign Service, but one Foreign Service officer who could write with rare power and lucidity was the late John Franklin Campbell, editor of the quarterly magazine *Foreign Policy* until his untimely death at 31 in November 1971. His book dissecting the State Department is entitled *The Foreign Affairs Fudge Factory*.

In his incisive discussion of the department's problems, Mr. Campbell puts full emphasis on the fact that it has suffered from a population explosion. It is simply too big, though greatly exceeded in numbers by other government instrumentalities that encroach on foreign policy, such as the CIA and the military. Though our embassies in every capital of the world are overstaffed, it is largely by personnel from other departments, bureaus, and agencies, since not more than 22 percent of the Americans on embassy staffs work for the State Department.

The major period of State Department expansion occurred during the war and in the immediate postwar years. Today it has hardly any more employes than it had in 1954, and, with that personnel, mans almost twice as many embassies as were then maintained. Yet the department could no doubt still improve its performance if it were leaner, and particularly if it were manned by more young and fewer middle-aged officers. The reason for the bulge in the middle years is a matter of history, since the service was tripled in size in 1956 by the lateral assimilation of Washington civil servants already in the State Department or drawn from other agencies.

A selective reduction in personnel makes not only administrative but substantive sense; it would tend to tailor our foreign policy apparatus to the requirements of a proper United States foreign policy. We are well past the evangelical days of the early 1960s, when there was a tendency to believe that the United States had only two really interesting tools of diplomacy: its ability to hand out economic aid, and its willingness to provide arms, or even troops, in support of governments prepared to resist invasion from without or subversion from within.

During that period, the question of subversion from within was given a theoretical respectability by Peking's promises of support for "wars of national liberation."

All this provided the grist for a new intellectual fad—or, as it came to be, an obsession—of which the underlying assumptions were not very complicated. We had learned how to live with Soviet efforts to foment communist revolutions in industrialized areas, but Maoism presented a novel problem, since it promised, by teaching and assisting in the techniques of guerrilla warfare in agrarian states, to spread its domination over what the French had poetically named the "Third World."

The amount of high-class intellectual effort applied to scriptual exegesis of the words of Lin Piao, Mao Tse-tung, and other high priests of "wars of national liberation" was—it seemed to me at the time— quite excessive. Classes in counterinsurgency were arranged without much regard to relevance. Though there was little chance that our envoy to the Court of St. James might encounter insurgents behind the trees in Hyde Park or that our man in Paris would be threatened by peasant cadres in the Place de la Concorde, new appointees to these posts were routinely scheduled for such classes.

All this was a passing phase, though it left a residue of debris in its wake. "Bureaucratic lag" is a well-known ailment that is now taking its toll, for just at a time when the nation needs a new crop of negotiators, we have in inventory a surplus of trained counterinsurgents and repatriated Peace Corps volunteers.

Yet, far more serious is the fact that we cannot regard the counterinsurgency craze as an isolated fad; it was part of the whole mania for over-intellectualizing the Vietnam War and surrounding it with a soap bubble of speculation and rationalization. Integrally related was the problem of "escalated rhetoric," which has, from the beginning, impeded the search for a sensible approach. If ever any subject might have profited from "benign neglect," it was our obsession with the endless nightmare struggle in the rice paddies.

No doubt we shall learn many things from Vietnam, but what will endure as the principal lesson remains to be seen, for no two people can agree on how to formulate it.

Perhaps it will be a reenforcement of Metternich's famous caution against too much zeal, because there is no doubt that our foreign policy during the 1960s was overly exuberant. We reacted to every new development, not because it might threaten our interests as a nation or erode our power position, but out of a sense of annointed mission to encourage good and resist evil wherever we might find it.

Today that pretension is pretty well played out. Our country is, I think, in a mood to reduce activities to the scale of our definable national interests—or even beyond. The danger is that we may shrink our involvement indiscriminately. That there is room for some highly selective shrinkage can hardly be questioned. During my years in the State Department I could never understand, for example, why our African Bureau passionately insisted that we should have the biggest embassy in the capital of every small African state, even though our ties with the people of that state had developed only recently and there were other nations with historic trade patterns, investments, and cultural relationships that clearly justified a larger involvement.

America is a volatile country and opinion as to our proper role in the world has suffered an abrupt change. A recent poll of twenty-five- to thirty-four-year-old "potential leaders" shows, for example, overwhelming agreement with this statement: "It is not clear that any development in Latin America, Africa, or

Asia (with the possible exception of Japan) would affect the security or vital interests of the United States."

Such an airy answer does not make me happy, since there is serious danger that we may swing through the full alphabet from zeal to apathy. Whether our "potential leaders" have scaled down their assessment of America's interests out of modesty, ignorance, or indolence is a matter of conjecture. What we need most of all is perception and balance, because there are many areas of the world where a strong and substantial United States presence is not only justified but imperative.

XIII

So far, in commenting on the manner in which we make and administer our foreign policy, I have discussed only the activities of the executive branch, and have not mentioned the foreign policy responsibilities of the Congress. That was not inadvertent but a reflection of the state of affairs that has existed ever since the Korean War, when America first began to deploy its power on every continent. Yet the president's dominance of foreign policy is today being challenged, and that cannot help but affect the State Department's own place in the cosmos.

For what they no doubt regarded as good and sufficient reasons, the Founding Fathers left ambiguous the respective roles of the legislative and executive branches in the area of foreign policy. Thus the Constitution confers on the president certain powers by which he can affect our foreign relations, while assigning certain other such powers to the Congress, and still others specifically to the Senate. The result has been to encourage a spirit of institutional free enterprise, with active competition between the two coordinate branches. Sometimes that competition has been restrained, or at least cushioned, by easy working arrangements between the president and leading personalities in the legislative branch. The halcyon time newspaper columnists automatically invoke with nostalgia was the period of the Eightieth Congress when Senator Vandenberg ruled the Senate Foreign Relations Committee.

The mistrust and antagonism prevailing today between the White House and key enclaves on Capitol Hill—notably the Senate Foreign Relations Committee—are a complex phenomenon. A conflict of personalities, or even of ideas, is by no means the whole story. The central focus of disagreement is on the role of Congress both in starting wars and in stopping them, but there is also a strong feeling that the executive branch has been less than candid in dealing with the Congress and has tried to practice thought control by withholding essential information.

Certainly there is a growing and increasingly passionate conviction in congressional circles that we should be stopping the Indo-Chinese War faster than we are presently. Compounding the disenchantment is resentment that Congress was never asked to declare the war, and suspicion that the Tonkin Gulf resolution was extracted under the duress of circumstances not adequately disclosed to the Congress at a time when the modest level of United States involvement gave little indication of the escalation that was to follow. Yet the postmortem now going forward makes it quite clear that if the executive was, in fact, guilty of presumptuous action—a sin of commission—then the Congress was guilty of complacent inaction—a sin of omission. Or, to move from theology to the vulgate, the executive got us into a mess, treating the Congress as its patsy.

It was inevitable, as conviction hardened on these points, that the Congress would seek to move the balance of power between it and the executive nearer the equilibrium that the Constitution intended.

Broadly speaking, the measures now proposed for this purpose are of two kinds. One would clarify the power to start wars; the other would seek to assure the ability of Congress to obtain the information needed in order to act as an effective check against the president.

Among the measures that would affect the legislative-executive balance are those relating to what one might call "Congress' right to know," or, indeed, "Congress' need to know." What the famous Pentagon Papers have disclosed, among other things, is how inadequately Congress was informed, not only as to the conduct of the war, but also as to the less optimistic assessments that from time to time prevailed in the executive branch.

Unquestionably, the relations between the two branches with regard to Vietnam—and more particularly with regard to the political aspects of the struggle—have been marked by a good deal of bickering—and, in the case of the Senate Foreign Relations Committee, downright bitterness. In fact, recent administrations have looked on the Foreign Relations Committee as an adversary against which it is justified in using tactics of silence.

For the moment, principal emphasis is on the practice of the executive branch in denying Congress access not only to particular kinds of information, but also to certain key administration functionaries on the ground of "executive privilege" or, as it is sometimes referred to, "executive immunity," or "executive secrecy." Whatever terminology is employed, the practice finds no serious support in the Constitution, constitutional history, statutory provisions, or judicial declarations. Its sole claim to legitimacy depends on its having been repeatedly asserted in self-serving statements of the president and other members of the executive branch over a great many years, thereby acquiring the dignity of usage.

The closest to a constitutional argument that can be made in support of the practice derives from those provisions giving the Congress the general power to legislate and delegating to the president the responsibility to ". . . take care that the laws be faithfully executed" (Article II, Sec. 3). In view of the fact that the Constitution provides a system of separation of powers, it is argued that neither branch may interfere in the internal workings of the other and thus Congress may not at will require the executive to produce documents and information which the executive feels should be withheld. On this tenuous contention some attorneys general have concluded that the president has the absolute discretion to determine what information and documents will be released to the Congress.

Though the logic denying such a conclusion is, to my mind, persuasive, the abstract issue has little place in an article concerned with the organization of the State Department. Indeed, I would not regard the question of executive privilege as relevant at all, had presidents not formed the habit of extending the claim of immunity to cover people as well as documents, by refusing to make members of the White House staff available for testimony before congressional committees.

Still, so long as presidents looked to the State Department for their principal foreign policy guidance no one cared very much. But President Nixon's penchant for relying for advice on the

White House "family," rather than on the traditional departments, could well produce a constitutional challenge of serious dimensions. It is not merely the ascendancy of Dr. Kissinger to the role of major foreign policy advisor that is likely to create the issue; the President has recently adapted the pattern of the National Security Council to other areas of policy as well. Thus, he has created the Domestic Council with a staff presided over by John D. Ehrlichman and has delegated the overall direction of foreign economic policy to still another council, with still another White House staff directed by Peter Peterson.

The result is to create a situation almost certainly guaranteed to lead to congressional disenchantment and ultimately to revolt. Thus the Senate Foreign Relations Committee has already made known its unhappiness at being denied the opportunity to have Dr. Kissinger testify on such matters, for example, as his trip to China, and, at a later time, when foreign trade policy again becomes a major issue, there will quite likely be further trouble; for I doubt that the relevant committees will be content to hear from lesser figures in the State and Commerce Departments, knowing that Mr. Peterson is the dominant official of the executive branch in the development and administration of the policies before them.

In the long run, I think it probable that congressional resistance to the application of executive privilege to members of the White House staff may prove the controlling element in halting the rapid evolution of a super-State Department in the White House. To be sure, a president could neutralize congressional objections by permitting his national security advisor, as well as his advisors on domestic and foreign economic policy, to appear before congressional committees. But, given the sensitivity of presidents to the preservation of their own prerogatives, that seems not likely to happen. For if the president's personal assistants are required to testify, then why not the president himself? Obviously, there is a logical answer to the question, but I find it hard to believe that any president would give it.

On the whole, the pressures on Congress to play a more direct and active role in foreign policy seem to me healthy, and it is heartening to observe a new alertness on the part of the key committees. One useful result of this is the migration of several gifted young foreign policy experts, not only from the State Department but also from the White House, to the staffs of congressional committees, and particularly the Senate Foreign Relations Committee. To some extent this may be interpreted as a vote of no-confidence in the executive branch. By the same token, it may well be the harbinger of a time when there will be a substantial redressing of the balance of responsibility in foreign affairs between the two ends of Pennsylvania Avenue.

If I were the president, I would take due account of the decision of these young men. They know the problem, and they sense where the winds are blowing.

XIV

What we have learned in the past few months is that it is impossible to conduct an effective foreign policy that does not correspond to the broad will and aspirations of the American people. In theory, at least, it is the members of Congress, sensitive as they must necessarily be to the votes of their constituents, who should be most aware of what the public wants.

Thus, it is intolerable that we should long continue with the prevailing disarray in the relations between the two coordinate branches in the area of policy most vital to our survival and fulfillment as a nation. Not only does this present a squalid appearance to the American people, but the lack of a sense of common purpose between the president and Congress weakens us in the tough competition of the international arena.

As with so many of our difficulties today, the agony of Vietnam is the festering center of the problem. Yet, how absurd it is to permit the whole foreign policy of the United States to turn on the peripheral issue of our involvement in a tiny, only marginally important, piece of real estate five thousand miles from our borders! Perhaps relations between the present administration and the Foreign Relations Committee have been eroded beyond repair; but I would remind the present administration that if they do not make a serious effort to regain the confidence of the Congress—and particularly of the Senate —with regard to foreign policy, they will be in a poor position to command congressional confidence and understanding when new crises occur that require vigorous, incisive American action.

And there will be many in the years ahead.

United States Policy in Europe

Denis Healey

ONCE UPON A TIME in the nineteenth century, there was a British foreign minister named Palmerston (who, among his many other distinctions, seduced one of Her Majesty's ladies-in-waiting when he was at a party in Windsor Castle). He was once asked what were the principles of British foreign policy. He replied that British foreign policy had no principles; it had only interests.

The United States did not have a foreign policy until 1945. In 1936 the Congress committed the United States to permanent neutrality by passing the Neutrality Act. When the United States did have a foreign policy in 1945, it was in the extraordinary situation of having no interests, only principles.

The post-war situation resulting from the destruction of the Second World War—the creation of a power vacuum between the United States and Russia, running from Europe through the Middle East and South Asia to Japan—meant that the United States felt herself called on to play the leading role in organizing what she described as the Free World. But the United States had very few direct national interests at stake in these areas that were subject, or were thought to be subject, to Communist pressure. So, in 1945, the first major American action of peacetime engagement in world affairs—a policy which she had previously renounced either under the protection of the Monroe Doctrine or under the compulsion of the Neutrality Act—namely President Truman's decision to take up the burden that Britain couldn't carry and wouldn't carry in Greece in 1947, was justified by a doctrine, the Truman Doctrine.

Over the following six or seven years in which United States post-war policy was crystallizing into a fairly systematic shape, America's attitude toward the outside world more and more was molded by a particular view of what the world was like and what America's role in it should be. Perhaps it is not always realized in the United States how rare is this approach to world affairs. Normally a country's foreign policy is determined by its interests, by an immediate threat to its national security, or by its economic needs. But in 1945 the United States had very few direct interests in the outside world, though she had many indirect ones. Consequently, she justified her interventionist policy by a general concept of what the world should be like. Her vision of the outside world was determined to a very large extent by the fact that the threat to the world order she had hoped would develop under the post-war organization of the United Nations came primarily from the Soviet Union.

The Soviet government, like the United States government, had a world policy which was determined to a very large extent by doctrine. Oddly enough, the Soviet doctrine and the American doctrine were two sides of the same coin. The Soviet version was probably best defined by one of Russia's leaders, Zhdanov, when the Cominform was created. It was the doctrine of the two camps. The Russians believed that the whole world would, in the end, be run in the same way as the Soviet Union because the decisive factor in world affairs was the class struggle. The class struggle was not just a national, but an international conflict. Sooner or later the proletariat all over the world would win power by revolution. Having won power under the leadership of Communist parties, they would look to the leadership of the Soviet Communist party for guidance, and inspiration. That was the Soviet view as defined by many Russian writers in the post-war period.

The American view was the complement of that. It was that we were unlikely ever to have world peace so long as there were countries that took the same world view as the Soviet Union. The real model for world order was a world governed by law in which national governments subjected their power in important respects to a world authority. The unwritten assumption, always, was that when this happy state of affairs came about, all countries would look at the world in very much the same way as the United States looked at it.

So far as Europe was concerned, most leading Americans strongly believed Europe would only recover from the damage of war and play an effective role in this new world order if she followed the American model and set up a federal constitution. The concept of Europe as a federal state in the American image was one of the elements in the American world view as it crystallized in the first decade after 1945. There was a very strong feeling in the immediate post-war period that not only the developed countries with Western civilizations, but even the countries of Africa, the Middle East, and Asia would, in the end, have to decide to follow either the Russian pattern or the American pattern. In this situation in which a fundamental conflict separated two visions of a world order—one represented and led by the United States and the other represented and led by the Soviet Union—neutrality would be impossible in practice. Also both sides thought it would be morally wrong.

It is odd, looking back, to recall how certain at that time Russian and American leaders were that their respective pictures of the world's development were sensible. In fact, of course, the world has in many respects followed a very different course in the last quarter of a century. Even now, when the illusion of American omnipotence, which helped to shape so much of American policy in the early years after the war, has been shattered by the tragedy of Vietnam, and an American president has decided to give up the role of the world's policeman, he has found it necessary to define the United States interest in disengagement in terms, like President Truman, of a doctrine—the Nixon Doctrine.

Yet I doubt whether this approach to world affairs in terms of doctrines is any longer very adequate. The world, twenty-five years after the end of the Second World War, is an infinitely more complex and intractable place than it was thought to be by either side in 1945. In fact, the United States is learning, as other countries have had to learn before her, that she cannot base a foreign policy either on pure principle or doctrine or on a crude conception of national interest. Any state has to have something between the two.

The approach of the American intelligentsia to world affairs in 1945 was the approach of the lawyer; it assumed that the world should be governed by law. It is not a very practical approach. Equally, the Soviet approach of 1945, the social engineering approach—the idea that people can be manipulated just as machinery can—that is not a practical approach either.

If a choice for a model of a profession to guide foreign ministers must be made, a better choice than either the lawyer or the engineer would be that of the gardener. A gardener has to accept certain intractabilities, for example in the soil in which he plants. He can change its nature a little bit by adding peat, or sand, or lime; but the soil creates certain limitations. He also has to accept the limitations created by the conditions required for the growth of certain plants. Even when he has adapted his plans as carefully as possible to the physical properties of the objects he is concerned with, he is up against changes in the weather. He has to be prepared continuously to adjust and shift. If he is sensible, he has to be prepared for continuous disappointments when the weather goes wrong. This sort of approach to world affairs is now and has always been the only one likely to enable governments to avoid appalling disappointments and disasters. It is certainly the only appropriate one today.

So much by way of very general background. Now a word or two about United States policy towards Europe over the last quarter of a century as a preface to what I have to say about United States policy toward Europe in the coming decades. First of all, the American approach to Europe in 1945, as I have already said, was dominated by the vision of a world split into two camps by the Cold War. The United States believed that Western Europe was threatened by the political spread of communism, aided and abetted by the military pressure of the Red Army which, as a result of the way the war ended, was standing on a line running from Stettin to Trieste. This situation was predicted, incidentally, by a journalist in the *New York Tribune* in 1848. His name was Karl Marx.

America had a two-pronged attitude towards the immediate problem:

1. To provide enough economic assistance to the countries of Western Europe to enable them to build societies which would be immune to the internal spread of communism;

2. To provide sufficient military protection of Western Europe along the Iron Curtain to prevent an external attack by the Red Army.

In fact, that two-pronged policy was astoundingly successful. A similar policy, applied to Japan in the Far East, was also astoundingly successful.

Unfortunately, however, this first step—the rendering of Western Europe immune to attack and immune to the spread of communism—was not followed by the second step: the creation of a West European Federation which many Americans hoped and thought in the late forties would enable the United States to retire from an active role in Europe altogether.

More important still, the attempt to apply the same policy to the world between Europe and Japan was a total failure. The attempt to protect the Middle East against communist penetration or Russian influence by the creation of the Baghdad Pact —an idea which was part British and part American—had exactly the opposite effect. It put the Russians into the Middle East for the very first time. SEATO never really got off the ground at all as a military organization. There is some truth in the saying of Professor John Kenneth Galbraith that the Third World— that part of the world lying between Japan and Western Europe and south of the Soviet Union—is the disaster area of American foreign policy.

Fortunately, however, the failures of American policy in this part of the world were not the successes of Soviet policy. Russia has made as much of a mess of her policy in Afro-Asia as the United States has. Just look, for an example, at the total failure of her policy in Indonesia. The really striking thing about the Third World is that it has shown no eagerness to be run from either Washington or Moscow. Indeed, it regards the Cold War as a monumental irrelevance. The war or the conflict which concerns the Third World more and more is the conflict between the rich, white people in the Northern Hemisphere—whether they are communist or capitalist—and the poor, mainly colored peoples to the south who are separated by a growing economic gap from the rich countries to the north.

By 1950, within five years after the end of the Second World War, the battle against the spread of communism had been won in Western Europe. NATO had been set up and the danger of a Soviet attack against Western Europe seemed to be receding. As a result of the extraordinarily successful operation of the Marshall Plan for giving American economic help to Western Europe, the West European countries had not only recovered their pre-war economic strength, but had gone far beyond it.

Partly as a result of this improved economic picture, the Communist parties which were gaining strength internally in the first year or two after 1945, steadily lost influence. The only two important Communist parties now in Western Europe are the parties in France and Italy. Neither of them believes that it has any chance at present of winning power by revolutionary means. The French Communist party is now so comfortable after its very long period as the opposition party that it has almost become France's version of Her Majesty's Opposition. It is surprising in some ways that its leaders do not receive state salaries like the leaders of the Opposition in Britain.

In Italy the Communist party is deeply divided on where to go. An important element in it believes that it ought to move towards the social democratic position. The most it hopes for is to enter a coalition government as a loyal national Italian party. The Italian Communist party was the first West European party to break away from Soviet leadership.

The one disappointment in Europe has come on the Mediterranean flank of Western Europe where economic recovery has not led to political democracy. Turkey has a most unique system including free elections and a large degree of internal democracy, but also an army that steps in and corrects course whenever it thinks the politicians are going wrong. Unlike most armies, it is content to do that, without trying to run the country itself. In Greece, however, the army has taken the country over entirely and is not making a great success of it from any point of view. In Spain, the peculiar system installed by General Franco at the end of the Spanish Civil War seems likely to last for quite a time in some form or another, even after Franco himself passes from the scene.

So much for the internal achievements of American policy—the establishment of robust, prosperous democracies in most of Western Europe and disappointment in some of the Mediterranean countries. On the other hand, so far as the military security of Western Europe is concerned, here American policy has been a total success. In 1949, all the Russians needed to get to the North Sea was boots. There was no military strength of any importance in Western Europe. Even when NATO was first set up, it was often described as being like the Venus de Milo because it was all SHAPE with no arms. Since then, NATO has built up a sizable conventional force in Western Europe and that, combined with America's nuclear guarantee, has not only protected Western Europe from a Soviet military attack, but has also given West Europeans a great sense of psychological security. People were really worried in the late fifties that the Red Army might come West. For that reason, businessmen in Germany and Italy were financing the Communist party in the hope that that would keep them off the lamp posts when the Red Army arrived. This type of insecurity has now completely disappeared.

The disappointments, as pointed out earlier, have come because after having achieved prosperity and security, Western Europe has not had the gratitude to follow the American model and federate. Indeed, although Western Europe now works infinitely more closely as an entity than anybody would have expected before the Second World War, it is appallingly slow to move towards even minor forms of supranational organization. Indeed, it has been well said that mythology was quite wrong in saying that Europa married a bull; she married a snail.

I believe myself that Americans were not realistic, even in terms of their own experience in history, in expecting Europe to federate quickly. Indeed, at the very moment when American politicians were pressuring the Europeans to federate, they were trying to hold up the admission of Alaska and Hawaii into the American federation for fear that admission might lead to a difference of one or two votes in the congressional balance. The Americans who pressed us to federate rarely recalled that the American federation led directly to the bloodiest civil war in history, in which the United States lost more men killed than in either of the world wars that followed—a fact that is more often recalled in Alabama than it is in Massachusetts.

Many attempts were made by American leaders to promote supranational solutions of problems. The European Defense Community was stillborne because the French would not accept it. The Multilateral Force was a project for satisfying non-nuclear Europe's demand for nuclear weapons by artificial dissemination. It failed as well; in fact, there was not much demand at the time for nuclear weapons in Europe; and such as there was has since been met satisfactorily in other ways.

Even more disturbing, I think, to some Americans has been

the fact that as Europe recovered strength, instead of agreeing automatically with the United States, it started disagreeing about quite a lot of important matters. By now most American political leaders have had the sense to realize that this was inevitable and in some ways even desirable.

The other theory which guided United States policy in the immediate post-war period is that once Europe had achieved strength and security, Communism in Eastern Europe would be "rolled back," to use Mr. Dulles' phrase. That, of course, has not happened. Nobody thinks now that it is conceivable that the West could use military force or the threat of military force to change the political situation in Eastern Europe. On the other hand, what has happened in Eastern Europe in the last fifteen years—indeed, it started with Tito's break-away from the Cominform in 1948—is that once Communist parties got state power outside Russia, they ceased to be obedient to the Soviet Communist party. Even though they disagreed with many of their fellow citizens on many economic and political matters, on the question of national independence, Communist leaders tended to take the same line as the rest of their populations.

In fact, Russia has had growing difficulty in controlling Eastern Europe over the last twenty years. Violent risings have occurred in East Berlin and Hungary. The Red Army was forced to intervene in Czechoslovakia. Trouble has erupted in some of the Polish cities. Rumania—surprisingly the country closest to the Soviet Union and least accessible to the West—has taken an independent line on foreign policy matters. Hungary, under Kadar, is taking an independent line on economic policy.

The situation today is significantly different from that expected a quarter of a century ago. Robust, prosperous, secure, confident countries in Western Europe are working more closely together than ever before, though moving very slowly, if at all, toward the sort of federal system which many Americans hoped to see. Tremendous turbulence exists in Eastern Europe; but there is no prospect whatever of Western Europe or NATO as a whole attempting to change the situation in Eastern Europe by military force or pressure. A very different situation prevails in much of the rest of the world, given the failure of the original American policy in Afro-Asia; and yet little advantage flows to the Russians from these failures.

So much for the last quarter of a century. I now want to discuss the future under three headings:

1. The security problem—the future of NATO and America's relationship with Western Europe and NATO.

2. The question of West European unity—what is going to happen over the Common Market and how will it affect United States policy?

3. The question of the division of Europe between East and West—what is going to happen about that and how is that going to affect United States policy?

First of all, NATO. NATO, like all political institutions, has become the object of a great deal of confusing rhetoric. NATO is not an institution whose object is to create heaven on earth. It has a much more limited objective, which is to prevent hell on earth. Since we have had hell on earth for most of the human population twice recently, if NATO can succeed in preventing hell on earth, if it can prevent a world war from starting yet again from a conflict in Europe, it will be worth the money and effort which we have invested in it.

NATO's success in preventing hell on earth has been quite extraordinary when we consider that the political tensions in Central Europe in 1945 and the decade following were probably more acute than Europe has known at any time in her previous history. On the one hand, Europe was divided against its will by the Iron Curtain. It was divided, moreover, across the middle of the most powerful country in Europe, Germany. That, in itself, in most previous centuries, would have been a certain recipe for war within twenty years. On top of that, the interstate conflict was aggravated by the ideological disagreements between the communist approach to the world and the Western approach to the world. Yet, at a time when the peoples of Africa, of Asia, and of the Middle East have known many wars, Europe has been totally immune from war between states, although we have had some bloody conflicts in Eastern Europe as the result of Soviet intervention in its internal problems. This is a great achievement, for which we should all be very grateful to NATO.

The way in which NATO has prevented war in Europe has been by convincing the Soviet government that if it used force to cross the Iron Curtain, it would be incurring an unacceptable risk of nuclear destruction. The original purpose of the West in setting NATO up in 1949 was to put Western Europe under the protection of America's nuclear power. Of course, the position has changed in many respects since then. In 1949, the United States could not drop nuclear weapons on Russia unless she had bases in Western Europe because the aircraft of that day did not have intercontinental range and there were no missiles. So America had an interest in offering Western Europe security in return for bomber bases and, in any case, had to protect her bases there. Moreover, the threat of nuclear retaliation was a very credible one in 1949 because at that time the United States had nuclear weapons and Russia had none. Here again, the situation has changed enormously. Russia's power to drop nuclear weapons on the United States is now roughly equal, for the first time, to America's power to drop nuclear weapons on Russia.

In that situation, it is not unnatural that the question is always being asked: will America really retaliate if Western Europe is attacked when the result of retaliation will be a Soviet nuclear attack on the United States? Although this question has often been asked, so far it has not critically reduced Western Europe's confidence in the American nuclear guarantee. This is partly because NATO has made great and successful efforts, particularly in the last five years, to revise its strategy so that America's liabilities are commensurate with the reduced stake she has in the security of Western Europe. We have done that in roughly three ways.

First, in 1967 NATO adopted a new strategy which was given the name of flexible response, although it had little in common with flexible response as defined by Mr. McNamara in 1963 or 1964. What flexible response means in current NATO strategy is that NATO will use whatever conventional forces it has in order to prolong the period of conventional resistance to the maximum. Now, that does not mean prolonging it a lot. If there were a large-scale conventional attack by the Soviet Union, Western Europe would be able to hold up the attack without using nuclear weapons for, say, four or six days instead of two or three, which was the situation in 1966.

The second change in NATO strategy is that which was adopted in the Nuclear Planning Group of NATO. Here there is an odd irony. Many people believe that Mr. McNamara set up the Nuclear Planning Group in order to persuade the Europeans that tactical nuclear weapons were useless. Perhaps that was Mr. McNamara's purpose; but in fact, the Europeans used the Nuclear Planning Group in order to find a way of using tactical nuclear weapons which America could accept— greatly to the chagrin of some of Mr. McNamara's advisors in the Pentagon. We now have a sensible, agreed way of introducing tactical nuclear weapons into a battle in Europe if we were faced with a scale of Soviet attack which we could not resist with our conventional forces.

The third new factor in the situation (although it is not entirely new) is that Britain and France now have small nuclear forces of their own—both strategic and tactical, although the French tactical weapons will not come into service for another two years. So, the Russian calculations about the possibility of a Western nuclear response are much less easy to make than they were when only the Americans had the power to decide. Yet, the Americans are not so worried about the French and British nuclear forces being used irresponsibly that they want to remove their own guarantee.

My personal opinion is that the NATO strategy as we now have it is sufficiently credible to satisfy the Europeans that they do not need to build up a big, independent nuclear force of their own for their security. At the same time, it is sufficiently rational to satisfy the United States that the risks it imposes on the United States are commensurate with America's interests in Europe.

But there are some problems ahead here. The effectiveness of the current NATO strategy depends on NATO having roughly the same conventional strength in Western Europe as it has now unless Russia reduces its forces in Eastern Europe. Two years ago, most people thought that the United States would make big cuts in her contribution to NATO as a result of the pressure exercised, for example, by Senator Mike Mansfield. As you know, President Nixon decided and announced in December 1970 that there would be no more cuts made—at least during his present term as president. After that some reduction in America's contribution is, in my view, more likely. The important thing is that before it takes place, the Europeans must be in a position to take up the slack; or, alternatively, we must have some confidence that we will be able to negotiate reciprocal reductions by the Warsaw powers in Eastern Europe.

During the last two years, Europe has already done a great deal to shift the burden from America to the other side of the Atlantic. For example, immediately following the Czech crisis in 1968, there were a lot of improvements made in NATO's military capabilities. Ninety percent of them were made by the European members of NATO rather than the United States, which was a unique situation in the history of NATO. In February 1971, with Britain's agreement to the European infrastructure program, we now have the European countries offering to pay about a billion dollars for improved infrastructure in order to relieve the United States of some of her current burdens.

The real question remains: is it possible to reduce the threat of war in Europe by agreement and cooperation between NATO and the Warsaw powers rather than by continued competition? Is there any chance, during the next ten years, of narrowing the gulf created at the end of World War II between Western and Eastern Europe?

This is a problem to which, not unnaturally, many Americans are very insensitive. When George Ball, for an example, wrote a very cogent article—with which I totally disagreed—in the Italian journal *Affari Esteri,* attacking Chancellor Brandt's Ostpolitik—he did not refer to the fact that the world has totally changed in the last twenty-five years. But, when we see what is happening in Poland, in Czechoslovakia, in Hungary, Western Europeans increasingly feel that the Iron Curtain means a mutilation of a culture—an impoverishment of Europe as a whole—which, if we possibly can, we want to end. For the people living in Western Germany, of course, the problem is very much more acute. There, separation from the inhabitants of Eastern Germany is something which, historically, is bound to be unacceptable; just as the partition of Poland is something which could never last, however often Poland was partitioned. And, of course, it creates special problems for the survival of Berlin as an island inside East Germany.

When the first stirrings of colonial revolt in Eastern Europe developed in the 1950s, the Russians had very few scruples about using military force to suppress them. We saw this in East Berlin as Soviet tanks were used to mow down German workers. We saw it in Hungary in 1956. Of course, in similar situations in similar periods, the great powers in the Western World were not very much more scrupulous. Britain and France tried unsuccessfully in 1956 to use military force to prevent President Nasser from nationalizing the Suez Canal. The United States tried, successfully, to use military force to prevent a change of government in the Dominican Republic.

But the world has changed a good deal in the last ten years. When the Russians faced a serious problem in Czechoslovakia in 1968, we know they debated for months about whether they could afford to use military force to suppress it. It was not until the weekend before the Russian tanks went in that they finally took the decision to do so.

When the riots took place in the Polish cities of Gdynia, Gdansk, and Sopot at Christmas time in 1970, the Russians made no attempt of any sort to intervene. Even more striking, they did not claim, as they always have on previous occasions, that the Polish workers were agents of Western imperialism who had been egged on by imperialist provocateurs. On the contrary, they acquiesced in the explanation honestly given by the Polish leaders that this had happened because the Communist party in Poland had failed to keep in touch with the workers. This is a tremendous change in attitude. I feel that the comparatively relaxed attitude of the United States towards the change of government in Chile is an equally encouraging shift in attitude on the Western side.

But the big question now is whether it is possible for the West to do anything which will encourage the Russians to come to terms with the movement for colonial freedom in Eastern Europe, the way Britain came to terms with the movement for colonial freedom in India, and other Western European countries finally came to terms with movements for colonial freedom in Indonesia, Algeria, and Indo-China.

Chancellor Brandt is attempting in his Ostpolitik to make one major contribution towards this by trying to persuade the Russians and the East Europeans that Western Germany genuinely wants to live at peace with her Eastern neighbors and will not attempt to take any military advantage of a change in the political relationship between Russia and Eastern Europe.

I believe that if we could get a European security conference which would set up continuing machinery for multilateral conversations between the Warsaw powers, the NATO powers, and the European neutrals, we might help to create a climate in which the Russians would be more ready to meet the legitimate demands of the East European countries for greater national independence.

If and when a European security conference meets, some of the technical problems about getting mutual reductions of forces will be as difficult as the problems faced by the Russian and American negotiators in the SALT talks about strategic arms limitations. But, equally, they are susceptible of solution if both sides genuinely want a solution. Just as I believe that the SALT talks will produce steady, but slow, progress on the limitation of strategic armaments, so I believe that a continuing dialogue between East and West on mutual force reductions in Europe would make progress. Indeed, I believe President Nixon is right to suggest in his 1971 Report to the Congress, "Building for Peace," that the SALT negotiations have produced an approach to arms limitations through "building blocks" which would be an equally valid approach for seeking European security.

I think one point of a very general nature is worth making here. It is very easy, remembering the appalling experiences of Western Europe after 1945, to look upon the Russians as devils whose only objective in life is to use any temporary military advantage they may have in order to enforce their will on the West. It is easy to do that; but it is not very rational to think that way.

At the moment, relations between Russia and the West, both in strategic nuclear terms and in terms of European security, are very stable. Neither side is really frightened that the other is going to attack it. It is inconceivable that the Russians would change the present situation by making a totally new agreement with the Western countries if they had the secret intention of cheating on the agreement in order to try to attack the West.

The risks they would run by pursuing such a course would be totally disproportionate to any advantage they could hope to gain.

I think if we look at this problem in terms of two groups of countries who disagree about an enormous number of problems, but who have common interests in the security field, then I think we will be a little more relaxed in our approach to them whether we are thinking of the SALT talks or of a European security conference.

I must now say a few words about the other major current aspect of relations between America and Europe—namely, the problems, opportunities, and challenges represented by the Common Market and what may happen to the Common Market in the next few years. At the moment, the Common Market or the European Economic Community, to use its proper name, contains six West European countries. There are three big ones: France, Germany, and Italy; two little ones: Belgium and Holland; and one that is very small indeed: Luxembourg.

At present, the Common Market is very far from having achieved the objectives it set for itself in the Rome Treaty. It is two things. First, it is a customs union for trade in industrial goods; there are now no customs barriers to trade in industrial goods between its members. Equally important, its common tariff against imports from the outside world is very low; so the creation of a customs union among these six countries has not reduced the trade between these countries and the outside world—exactly the contrary. Britain's and America's trade with the Common Market countries has gone up in the last twelve years almost as fast as the trade among the Common Market countries themselves. So, there are no real problems for the United States so far in this respect.

Secondly, it is a managed market in agricultural goods. Broadly speaking, the common agricultural policy of the Common Market involves, first of all, subsidizing agricultural production among the six countries concerned so that the farmers can sell their goods at a price which gives them a good return. It involves, secondly, putting levies on agricultural imports from the outside world so as to raise the price of foreign farm goods to the price created by the common agricultural subsidies inside the Common Market.

Some of the people who set up the common agricultural policy saw it primarily as a way of encouraging inefficient farmers in the Common Market to move into industry. Up to a point, it has had this result. The number of people dependent upon agriculture inside the Common Market has fallen from 23 percent of the working population in 1960 to 14 percent in 1970. It is hoped it will fall to 8 percent by 1980. Unfortunately, the price support policy has, even so, led to an enormous over-production of agricultural goods inside the Common Market. Until the Common Market started dumping its butter abroad at ridiculously low prices, the mountains of butter inside the Common Market which could not be consumed there threatened to assume Alpine proportions. The amount of money which is spent on subsidizing these unnecessary surpluses has become very large, too.

The Common Market now faces two great problems. The first is to make better sense of the common agricultural policy, which is not only imposing large economic burdens on everybody who is not a farmer in the Common Market, but is also infuriating people like the Americans outside the Common Market who can produce goods much more cheaply and would like to export them to Europe.

Secondly, EEC wants to go beyond the ordinary customs union already set up in industrial goods to develop common economic policies in every field. The trouble is that the French government will not agree to any supranational arrangements which include France. The result is that progress toward common policies is very difficult—in fact, almost non-existent. On this issue, there is no difference between President Pompidou and former President de Gaulle.

The German government, too, is cautious about moving too fast toward supranational policies because doing so might inhibit its efforts to bridge the gulf between Western Europe and Eastern Europe. In fact, none of the member countries is yet ready to surrender the right finally to veto a proposal it finds contrary to an important national interest.

At the moment, the two main proposals are not very worrying to anybody. On the political side, there is the so-called Davignon Proposal that the foreign ministers of the Common Market countries should meet twice a year for a chat. Well, fine, if they do; but doing so will not change the world.

The other proposal is the Werner Plan for a currency union. If the plan were adopted, it would mean that in 1980 a common currency would prevail throughout the Common Market. Now a common currency is possible only if common taxation policies are also in effect. The Werner Plan means that in 1980 the Sicilian land owner will have to pay the same tax rate as honestly as the Dutch businessman. Anybody who believes that this is possible by 1980 will believe anything. Nevertheless, a lot of people do want much closer cooperation on currency matters. Agreement was reached in February 1971 to take the first step toward closer cooperation on currency matters on the condition that if the French do not agree within three years to take a second step, the deal may be off.

This at least means that a little movement is possible. I do not believe that rapid movement towards economic union—still less, political union—is likely, whether it is desirable or not.

The other big challenge facing the Common Market is one of great concern to Britain. That is to enlarge the Common Market so that it includes a number of other countries that are prepared to accept the obligations that it imposes. So far, four of them have offered to do so—Britain, Denmark, Norway, and the Republic of Ireland. Moreover, the other European countries which are in the European Free Trade Area want a closer relationship with the Common Market than they have now, although for various reasons they do not want to join as full members. Austria, Sweden, and Switzerland, for examples, are neutral countries and do not therefore want to accept the political obligations of full membership. Portugal is too weak to accept the economic obligations.

Here again, the big problem has been the attitude of the French government. It is now clear that there is certainly a big difference between Monsieur Pompidou and General de Gaulle on the question of Britain joining the Common Market. General de Gaulle was opposed in principle to Britain joining the Common Market. Therefore, he did not mind on two occasions taking the blame for keeping us out. He imposed the veto when Mr. Macmillan applied. He imposed a veto when Mr. Wilson applied. President Pompidou is not opposed in principle to Britain's joining and he is determined not to take the blame for keeping us out. But until the upset over Nigeria and his row over currency with Germany it did not seem that he was prepared to pay the price for getting Britain in. The structure of the Common Market as it now exists was determined very largely by a group of brilliant French civil servants who dominated the negotiations which led to the Rome Treaty. The result was that the structure was a delicately articulated balance in which, on almost all issues, France's interests were well taken care of. In the end, President Pompidou changed his position and cleared the way for Britain's entry, but only after receiving assurances from Mr. Heath that Britain saw Europe's role in the world in the same way as France did, and after being offered a large British contribution to the support of the French-designed common agricultural policy.

The failure of the Common Market to turn into a federation, and some aspects of Common Market policy—particularly after Britain goes in—have begun to worry many Americans. A lot of Americans took the view that the United States should be willing to pay a price in order to get a European federation. But, if Western Europe is not going to achieve more than a loose relationship between countries, they do not see why American farmers should have to pay for it. There has been a good deal of strain between the United States and the Common Market on the Common Market agricultural policy. There are further strains developing because the Common Market wants to make private trading arrangements with a lot of countries in the underdeveloped world, not only ex-colonies of France, but even countries like Indonesia, which was once a colony of Holland. Some Americans fear that this would cut across the general approach which the United States wants to take toward trade between the rich and the poor countries. My own feeling is that none of these difficulties needs to require any basic change in America's policy of cooperation with Western Europe and encouragement of the enlargement and deepening of the community.

What really is important is something that does not directly affect American-European relations, i.e., that further steps should be taken in the immediate future on the whole question of freer trade in the non-Communist world. One of the reasons why the Common Market did not create any real problems for the countries outside it was that, under President Kennedy, a great round of mutual tariff reductions was agreed among all the developed countries in the world. But the developed world is beginning to face an increasing problem because the Japanese economy is growing at three or four times the rate of the American and European economies. Consequently, it is generating an enormous surplus of goods for export. Last year the Congress considered a bill which would have required some raising of tariffs against textile imports into the United States. Because of the change in the balance of forces and the mid-term election, that bill has collapsed; but it may be revived.

The developed world has an enormous interest in adjusting its trade policies so that the growing Japanese export surplus can be absorbed. If not, then the frustration of Japanese exports could lead to all sorts of disadvantageous changes in Japanese policy. Pressures to divert this production into arms would increase, and whatever one's view of the need for a higher Japanese defense budget, no on would want this to come about as a result of a severe disappointment with the West. Worse still, we could get a trade war developing right through the Western world from which all of us would suffer. A great deal, therefore, now depends on whether President Nixon is prepared to take the lead, perhaps this year, in proposing a new attempt to improve the prospects for growing mutual trade throughout the developed world.

I have spent some time discussing the attitude with which the West approached the immediate problems of the post-war period from 1945 to 1950 and trying to describe the world outlook which crystallized during the first decade after the war. I have also spent a little time on showing how totally different the world is today from what it was in 1945, and even more, from what we expected it to be by 1970 when we were looking at the future in 1945.

In the first place, there are no longer two camps in the world. The Soviet camp was split wide open by the defection of China, by the break-away of the East European countries, and by the refusal of foreign Communist parties to agree automatically that everything Russia says is right.

In the Western world, the relationship between Western Europe and the United States inevitably changed to a more equal one with the recovery of Western Europe from the damage of the war. The Third World is very intractable, both for the Western world and the Communist world. It has its own problems which it wants to solve in its own way. The Russians are no more successful than we are; and the Chinese are no more successful than the Russians in getting what they want in the Third World.

Perhaps the most important change is that all sorts of factors have enormously reduced the incentive for developed countries to use war as a means of increasing their influence vis-a-vis one another. We have an infinitely more complicated world today than we had in 1945. Thank God, on the whole, it is a much safer one.

For all these reasons, the countries of Western Europe are likely to be more concerned with the manifold problems of their own continent and its immediate neighbors during this decade. The six members of the Common Market have not found it easy to make the community machinery work. In some respects an enlarged community will result in even greater internal difficulties. For many years the best brains in the governments of Western Europe will have to concentrate a large proportion of their time on adjusting the community institutions to accommodate the new members and in reaching the compromises on which further progress depends.

I do not think it is always realized how much the policies of governments can be effected by the critical shortage of time available to handle the great variety of problems facing them. The relationship between Western Europe and Eastern Europe, not only in the field of military security but also in various fields of economic, social, and cultural cooperation, will also take a large proportion of the time available. Beyond that, Europe's interest in the Third World is likely to be directed more towards the problems of North Africa and the Middle East than towards Asia and Latin America, partly because geographical proximity dictates this, partly because of Europe's paramount need for oil.

It would not be reasonable to expect the European countries to play a military role in the Pacific or Indian Ocean areas, although they will be no less active than today in trade and investment there.

It is idle for Americans to complain of this; after all, American pressure was a major factor in accelerating Europe's withdrawal from empire in the decade after the war—and rightly so. America cannot now expect to push Europe back. American pressure was also an important factor in prompting the move towards greater European unity even if it was not always wisely or discreetly applied. The United States must accept the consequences of a greater unity in Europe. It has been hard work to keep the European movement going; it will be equally difficult to keep it on the move. Regrettable as it may be, unity in any social group is rarely achieved except at the cost of stressing separateness from other groups; for example, Britain's belated acceptance of a European destiny involved a fundamental psychological reorientation which is bound to reduce her interest in the areas east of Suez.

On the other hand, a uniting or united Europe will be as dependent as a divided Europe on a sensible ordering of international affairs so as to achieve a world in which all the nations can prosper in peace. In tackling the problems of world organization, whether in the field of trade or arms control, the United States can and must count on continuing a close cooperation with Europe.

In this new world into which we are now moving, I think the relationship between Western Europe and the United States will be a keystone of policy for both Western Europe and the United States. On the whole, for a variety of reasons—some connected with history and tradition and some connected with interests— the Western Europeans and the United States do tend to look at most world problems in the same sort of way. But the relationship will be much more equal in the future than it has been in the past.

The important thing is that in pursuing this new partnership, very different from the client relationship of the first ten years after the war, we recognize that most of the important problems are not the problems of our own relationship with one another. In this sense the partnership between Europe and the United States will succeed best when it is looking not inward but outward at the world as a whole.

Near-Sightedness in the Near East

Arnaud de Borchgrave

WHILE VIETNAM IS STILL our most anguishing problem, as President Nixon put it recently, the Middle East is still the most dangerous one. The Arab-Israeli conflict has the grim distinction that it can draw Soviet policy and our own into a collision course that could prove uncontrollable.

The Middle East's strategic location astride three continents, and its oil, about two-thirds of the world's total reserves, have combined to make the area a center of vital interest for all major powers, which has never been the case in Vietnam.

The Middle Eastern conflict has poisoned America's relations with the Arab world, which contains the oil jugular of both Western Europe and Japan, our two principal allies, and allowed Russia to become the dominant foreign influence in the Near East—a goal that has eluded Moscow for centuries.

Passions aroused by the Palestine question—now known as the Arab-Israeli conflict—have blurred facts and distorted history beyond recognition. Sentiment, legend, propaganda, all have thrown up a convenient smokescreen which makes it increasingly difficult to distinguish between American and Israeli interests.

Few objective voices have spoken out over the years. United States media seldom do the Arab case justice. Press, radio, television, movies, theater have conditioned public opinion into believing that all the good guys are in Israel on our side while all the bad guys are in the Arab countries on Russia's side.

I personally covered the Six-Day War from the Israeli side and I have no shame in admitting that I lost all sense of objectivity as I shared the life of this great citizen's army on three different fronts in less than a week. But if we allow our critical faculties to become clouded by an emotional commitment, we are in serious trouble.

Perhaps I could contribute to a little enlightenment by moving behind the scenes on two crucial exchanges between Arabs and Israelis during the last two years in which I was personally involved on *Newsweek's* behalf. After I had lobbied in Cairo for three weeks early in 1969, the late President Nasser agreed to see me and spelled out, for the first time since the Six-Day War, what he would be willing to give Israel in return for the evacuation of the occupied territories—namely recognition of Israel's territorial integrity and freedom of navigation in the Suez Canal and in the Straits of Tiran.

I then flew to Israel, by way of Rome, and offered the late Prime Minister Levi Eshkol a deal: he could see Nasser's very important remarks a week before publication provided he agreed to reply through *Newsweek* the following week. He agreed.

Rambling and discursive as he was prone to be, Eshkol answered my questions for two and one-half hours. Over and over again, he insisted on going back through two thousand years of Jewish history. When I respectfully suggested that he was not addressing himself to the points made by Nasser, he got very excited and said, "Now who's giving the interview, you or me?" When I asked him whether Israel would give up its new settlements in the occupied territories, as part of a final peace agreement, he told me he did not answer "iffy" questions.

A few hours later I returned to Eshkol's office to submit an abbreviated transcript, tailored to fit eight *Newsweek* columns, for the prime minister's final approval. This is the procedure I try to follow for interviews with statesmen that deal with such life-and-death issues. The next day, Eshkol's closest aide called and suggested what he described as an "optional insert"—something the prime minister had said but that I had left out as it seemed like a statement of the obvious and there simply was not enough space to publish all his utterances.

The insert in question read, "We Israelis do not want any part of the inhabited area of Jordan's West Bank"—Nablus, Jenin, Hebron, etcetera. Well, to say that you do not want cities that do not belong to you had not struck me as much of a concession. Yet this was the phrase that unleashed a political storm of major magnitude in Israel. There was an acrimonious debate in Parliament, a motion of no-confidence against the government, and

Eshkol himself suffered a heart attack that led to his final demise a few days later.

Eshkol was accused by some of his own ministers of giving away in one sentence in *Newsweek* the fruits of Israel's great military victory in 1967. With its back against the wall, the government deliberately lied and announced in Parliament that the incriminated sentence was not in the original text as submitted by me—thus making me out to be the culprit. It was not in the original for the simple reason that Eshkol himself had inserted it later.

I mention this because I think it refutes the thesis that the Arabs are the only ones inflexible and responsible for the deadlock in the quest for peace. If the truth be known, many prominent Israelis say off-the-record that the present ceasefire lines are the best borders they will ever have. And believers in this school of thought are determined to find any pretext to stay put.

To the Arabs, incidentally, the Eshkol-*Newsweek* incident was but one more piece of evidence that the Israelis are indeed expansionist.

My most recent attempt to promote a fresh dialogue between President Sadat and Prime Minister Golda Meir began shortly before the end of the last ceasefire period at the beginning of February. I arrived in Cairo in the midst of a government-generated war psychosis, ranging from mock air raid drills to convoys of Soviet-supplied missiles that kept driving by the Nile Hilton.

To my horror I discovered there were ninety-two other newsmen in town and that fourteen major publications and networks, most of them American, had made formal applications to see President Sadat. I typed out personal letters to the regime's six most important personalities, then hired the biggest limousine I could find in Cairo—a vintage Cadillac—to make myself look as important and as official as possible, and drove to Sadat's town residence at 6:30 in the morning. The private addresses of ministers are classified information in Egypt so I told the duty officer that I had very important messages from Washington to deliver. To my astonishment, he dutifully wrote down the six addresses in Arabic for the benefit of my driver. If I had sent the letters to the ministeries concerned they never would have reached the desks of the ministers. Word soon filtered out that no one was anxious to help me as the regime was still sore about a cover story I had done for *Newsweek* in the spring of 1970 on the Soviet missile buildup.

I kept bombarding the homes of the ministers with letters and after a week three of them agreed to see me. I pleaded that the time had come for Egypt to say publicly that it was willing to sign a peace agreement with Israel. I also dwelled on the evils of resuming shelling across the canal after February 5th, the end of the ceasefire period, because, as I put it, this would play right into the hands of certain Israeli hawks and trigger a fourth round that Egypt could not possibly win—and would most probably lose.

I told them how I thought President Sadat could win his spurs as one of the world's great statesmen by making peace with Israel and becoming a sort of Willy Brandt of the Arab world. Everyone seemed interested in my arguments and presumably some of the ministers got Sadat to listen, because a week later I was informed that the president had agreed to see me in principle—but that they couldn't tell me when and asked me to wait in my room for the call. I didn't leave the hotel for another eight days and, finally, the presidential summons arrived. I was to have lunch with Sadat the next day at his country place, an hour's drive north of Cairo.

We spent three hours together. And it was immediately obvious that this was to be a very important occasion. For the first time in a generation, an Egyptian leader was willing to say, for the record, that Egypt was willing to enter into a peace treaty with Israel, provided, of course, Israel evacuated the occupied territories.

It was a revolutionary break in doctrine and ideology. At an Arab summit meeting in Khartoum, right after the 1967 war, Arab leaders solemnly pledged "no peace . . . no recognition . . . and no negotiations." And now Sadat was telling me what he was willing to put in a peace treaty—namely the territorial inviolability and political independence of Israel. Sadat also dropped the right to return to Israel as an option for the Palestinian refugees—the first time an Arab leader had ever dared to concede the permanent reality of Israel as a purely Jewish state. He did not discount minor frontier changes in Israel's favor and guaranteed free passage for Israeli ships in the canal and in the straits with a Security Council-backed international peacekeeping force at Sharm el Sheik. Sadat's concessions prompted one leftwing Beirut paper sarcastically to editorialize, "The only thing he hasn't agreed to do is travel to Jerusalem himself to sign a formal act of surrender."

I returned to the Nile Hilton with thousands of words of notes, quickly typed up a script that would fit into six *Newsweek* columns and drove back out to Sadat's country residence to get his signature on the final text. He read it carefully for twenty minutes and suggested only two minor corrections. By the time I returned to the hotel, there was only one hour left until plane time. Donald Bergus, the head of the United States diplomatic mission, was waiting for me. He thought the interview was so important he wanted to cable the full text to Washington on an eyes-only basis for President Nixon, Henry Kissinger, Secretary Rogers, and Joseph Sisco. This was the only way of ensuring against leaks at the Washington end before *Newsweek* came out four days later.

With a prearranged code, I had already alerted New York to advise Jerusalem to inform Golda Meir that I was coming in from Cairo (via Zurich) and that she could have an advance copy of Sadat's remarks provided *Newsweek* would be the channel used for reaction and reply. She agreed.

Predictably, Mrs. Meir was very skeptical. I relayed a private message from the United States diplomatic representative in Cairo who felt this was a now-or-never moment to make peace and that further progress was now contingent on her own response. She was not impressed. She said she had heard this now-or-never line before and when I told her that Sadat could not go any further without being stabbed in the back by other Arab capitals, not to mention political rivals at home, she said matter-of-factly, "that's his problem."

The formal part of the interview—and I shall explain shortly why it was not the one that appeared in *Newsweek*—consisted of the prime minister casting doubts about Sadat's sincerity, instead of giving him the benefit of the doubt, and asking repeatedly, "Is he or is he not willing to sign a peace treaty with Israel?" When I told her this was clear in the interview, she said, "not clear enough."

Before leaving Jerusalem I warned the prime minister that her answers might appear a little out of date if Sadat, before her own interview appeared, were to confirm, through Ambassador Jarring, everything he had told *Newsweek* the week before. She seemed to think there was no chance of this happening.

Yet two hours after I left Tel Aviv for Europe, that is precisely what happened and Golda Meir was left with no alternative but to ask one of her aides to call *Newsweek* in New York and request that the interview be killed and that I return to Israel for a second interview. And that was the reason why the Sadat and Meir interviews did not run in consecutive issues, as I had originally planned.

In the second version she was still extremely negative, did not respond in any positive way to Sadat, and said quite openly that some of the border changes Israel requires may be regarded as major ones. Mrs. Meir says privately she does not trust the Egyptian offer. Well, there are ample reasons—and ample precedents—for not trusting Egyptian moves. But the suspicion was almost certainly misplaced this time. For no Egyptian government is going to suggest making peace with Israel for the sake of propaganda. Every Arab regime has avoided making such a statement for a quarter of a century. Sadat took a big chance talking about a peace treaty. He, too, has his hawks. From the intransigent hierarchy of the Arab Socialist Union to disaffected younger field grade officers, there is no shortage of political head-hunters waiting to push Sadat out should Israel continue to stand pat (witness the abortive attempt to depose the Egyptian president). But Sadat took a calculated risk for the sake of peace and it is a tragedy that Israel did not respond in kind. Once again, there is talk of the inevitability of battle in Cairo's official circles and an unprecedented chance for peace is slipping through the world's fingers.

If you look at Sadat's situation—and Egypt's circumstances—it is obvious that peace is in his interest. Another war would almost certainly bring another defeat—despite Soviet weaponry. And another defeat would place Sadat under further obligation to the Russians. On this particular front, Egyptian leaders feel the relationship is already far too close for comfort. The summer 1971 pro-Communist coup and anti-Communist counter-coup in the Sudan, and Egypt's part in defeating the Sudanese Communists, was a clear indication of how Sadat feels about the Communist threat in the Middle East.

There is, of course, an understandable reluctance in Israel to abandon present ceasefire lines. Many influential Israelis feel the canal is the best anti-tank ditch in the world. Almost four years of occupation have hardened, perceptibly, into feelings of ownership. Israelis have grown accustomed to the sense of security brought by the occupation of vast tracts of Arab land. Moshe Dayan recently called for more Israeli settlements in the West Bank, in Sinai, and on Golan. Israelis are very much engaged in the business of what they themselves call "creating facts"—a euphemism for permanent ownership.

To obtain real peace, however, inevitably a price has to be paid. So Israelis find it easier to dismiss Sadat's offer as illusory rather than adjust themselves to the idea of withdrawal. And with their dilatory tactics, they are merely making sure that Sadat's offer does indeed become illusory. A self-fulfilling prophecy may thus come true.

Israel has always said that the main stumbling block to peace was Egypt's refusal to give them a peace treaty. Now that that stumbling block has been removed, Israel is already raising new objections and setting new conditions. If this continues, we will be missing the first real opportunity for peace in a generation. And a major diplomatic clash between the United States and Israel and/or a fourth round in the Arab-Israeli war will become all but inevitable. This is clearly Ben-Gurion's conclusion. The former prime minister and one of Israel's founding fathers has advocated withdrawal from all territories, except East Jerusalem and the Golan Heights, and is willing to settle for an international force at Sharm el Sheik.

America's main interest is in preventing another war and in circumscribing Soviet influence in the Middle East as much as possible. The longer Israel stays put, however, the better the odds for war and this time with the attendant risk of a confrontation between the United States and the Soviet Union. In a recent editorial, the *New York Times* went so far as to criticize Senator Javits for ignoring "modern realities in suggesting that geography can be equated with security in the nuclear-missile age," and added: "The best way to reduce Soviet influence and to promote American interests in the area, to safeguard Israel's survival and to avert a big power confrontation that would be disastrous for everyone is to press for peace in accordance with the Security Council Resolution of November 22, 1967, backed by strong international guarantees." It is still not too late for the United States to recoup its losses in the Middle East and restore some balance with the Soviet Union in the Arab world—and perhaps help prevent yet another round of fighting between Arabs and Israelis. But this requires a more flexible United States attitude—not in its commitment to defend Israel, which no one questions, not even the Egyptians at this point, but in our apparent willingness to condone, or unwillingness to condemn, Israel's continued occupation of Arab lands.

President Nixon took a major step in this direction last March. He said Israel would have to return to the June 1967 borders with "minor adjustments." Secretary of State William Rogers followed this up with some personal arm-twisting in Jerusalem. But the only result was an acrimonious exchange with an unyielding Golda Meir. The United States was not willing to go so far as to make further aid to Israel conditional on withdrawal from the Suez Canal. Somehow the limits of United States flexibility are set by internal political considerations—and are reached before Israel begins to show any real flexibility itself.

A rudimentary grasp of the historical background of the Palestine case is indispensable to understand the present impasse. Until World War I, there was no Palestine problem. The Arabs represented the overwhelming majority of the population when the British seized Palestine from the Turks. In 1914 Palestine comprised some 690,000 people (85,000 of them Jews, the rest, or 88 percent, Arab). By the end of the First World War, the Jewish population had even fallen to 56,000. Epidemics, emigration, and deportation had taken their toll. Jews at that point represented no more than 9 percent.

Britain's contradictory policies, designed to placate both Arabs and Jews, began with the so-called McMahon correspondence in 1915. The British were anxious to enlist Arab support in the war against the Turks. Sharif Hussein of Mecca, the then chief Arab spokesman, negotiated terms under which Arabs would cooperate. In a nutshell, they wanted to make sure they would get their independence after the war. The British agreed and spelled out the areas that would be specifically excluded from independence. Palestine was not among them.

But it wasn't long before the British reneged. Zionist lobbyists in London were pulling hard in another direction. Dr. Chaim Weizmann was lecturing on chemistry at Manchester University and fortuitously enjoyed a residence in the constituency of Arthur Balfour, then British foreign secretary. The two men had become friends and cultivated a close intellectual relationship. Weizmann quickly realized how British imperialism could service the cause of Zionism. Blessed with a powerful personality, Weizmann widened his circle of influential contacts in the British government, making clear he would guarantee Zionist backing for a British protectorate in Palestine in return for an expression of official support for Jewish aspirations in Palestine.

The campaign paid off handsomely on November 2, 1917, when Arthur Balfour wrote a letter to the British Zionist Federation. The Balfour Declaration was born. It imposed on the British an insoluble dilemma. Jewish immigrants were introduced in such numbers that the Arabs felt threatened—and betrayed. Three Arab-Israeli wars later the problem is still basically the same.

The British had not only negotiated pledges to both Arabs and Jews; they were also negotiating with France and Russia on the final disposition of the Ottoman Empire. Perfidious Albion was not entirely to blame. There was an astonishing lack of coordination between the different departments concerned in London. No single minister was fully versed in the three sets of negotiations—with the Arabs, the Jews, and the powers. Apparently no one realized that the non-Jewish communities referred to in Balfour's Declaration represented almost 90 percent of the people of Palestine.

The British had undertaken an impossible task—to establish a national home (but not a state) for the Jewish people in Palestine without jeopardizing the rights of the Arab majority. It was hardly surprising, therefore, that British policy constantly oscillated between the two contradictory provisions of the mandate. In his memoirs, Sir Ronald Storrs, one of the first British administrators in Palestine, wrote that "two hours of Arab grievances drive me into the synagogue while after an intensive course of Zionist propaganda I am prepared to embrace Islam."

In 1918, Weizmann went to Cairo and Jerusalem and pledged to Arab leaders that Zionist plans for Jewish migration to Palestine would not prejudice Arab rights. He told Palestine Arab leaders that the aim of the Jews was to work side by side with the Arabs, not seek political power.

During the Paris Peace Conference in 1919, President Wilson suggested that an allied commission should be sent to the Mideast to determine the aspirations of the Palestinian people. The King-Crane Commission (named after its two American members after Britain and France dropped out rather than face recommendations adverse to the Zionists) returned with a report that Wilson never actually saw (because of his collapse) and which finally joined the archives of the State Department.

The unlimited immigration of Jews, the commission said, would eventually turn Palestine into a Jewish state which would constitute the "gravest trespass" against the rights of the majority Arabs who were "emphatically against the entire Zionist program." The nub of the commission's recommendations: a "serious modification of the extreme Zionist program" of unlimited immigration.

Zionist ambitions were growing rapidly. In a memorandum submitted to the same Paris Peace Conference, they asked that Palestine's borders be extended northward to Sidon, on Lebanon's Mediterranean coast, eastward into Syria across Mount Hermon to the Hijaz railway and southward to Aqaba. In 1920, when an Arab delegation visited London to seek clarification on British aims in Palestine, they were astonished to find themselves referred by the government to Zionist headquarters. As J. Rives Childs, former United States ambassador to Saudi Arabia, says in his *Foreign Service Farewell,* "obtruding with growing persistence was a factor which was to prove controlling in the eventual settlement of the Palestine problem . . . the relentless pressure of American Zionists on the British government, exercised through the American government, looking to the implementation of the provision of the mandate which favored a Jewish National Home and ignoring the second—safeguarding the rights of the Palestinian Arabs. This Zionist pressure in the end was decisive in dictating both American and British foreign policy toward that country."

In September 1922, President Harding signed a joint resolution of both houses of Congress endorsing the Balfour Declaration—an indication of the growing influence of Zionism in United States domestic politics. By then a Zionist Congress in the Hague had disclosed the movement's real aims for the first time: "national state" was substituted for "national home" and Weizmann said the Zionists intended to make Palestine "just as Jewish as America is American and England is English."

The Mandate for Palestine, a de facto arrangement since 1917, was finally approved by the League of Nations in 1923. It made Britain responsible for "placing the country under such political, administrative, and economic conditions as will secure the establishment of the Jewish National Home"; it encouraged "close settlement by Jews of the land," while protecting the undefined rights of the other unidentified sections of the population; authorized facilities for Jewish immigration and the establishment of a Jewish agency to help Britain on all matters pertaining to the creation of a national home. The Zionist organization was empowered to become that agency. Hebrew was also authorized, along with English and Arabic, as an official language. Sir Herbert Samuel, Britian's choice for high commissioner, became the first Jew to rule Palestine in thirteen hundred years. He warmly supported the Zionists and had visions of four million Jews settled in Palestine.

All this occurred less than one year after Britain formally denied that the purpose of the mandate exercise was to create a completely Jewish Palestine. The British had even made clear that a Jewish national home, found in Palestine, and a Jewish state were entirely different matters. But the mandate itself, under Zionist pressure, was decidedly Zionist-oriented. And in Palestine, the Jews, supported by Zionist organizations and so much more advanced educationally than the Arabs, soon grew into a state within a state.

The Jewish Agency became a sort of executive and held effective power for immigration and land settlement. The nascent state's body politic was completed with an embryonic Parliament (Vaad Leumi), a trade union, and a military branch (Haganah). It had even been agreed among the Jewish leaders that when the Jewish state was officially established, Weizmann would be president and Ben-Gurion prime minister.

Massive Jewish immigration touched off widespread Arab disorders. There were major clashes between the two communities as early as 1929. Between 1936 and 1937, Arab losses were over 1,000 dead versus 82 Jews. By 1939, on the eve of World War II, the toll had mounted to 3,500 Arabs killed compared with 250 Jews and 77 Britons.

The British tried to correct the balance by imposing checks on the influx of Jews. American Zionists promptly flooded the State Department with letters and cables—a hundred thousand in a week—appealing to the United States government to intervene. Virtually identical telegrams gave some indication of the inspired nature of the campaign. Rives Childs says "it was undoubtedly the greatest [pressure campaign] ever brought to bear on the American government on any foreign issue." Equivocal United States response unleased a new wave of pressure—this time from a dozen state governors and 100-odd Congressmen. It was the first attempt to intimidate irresolute politicians by the threat of withholding votes and party contributions at the command of the Zionist organization.

Secretary Hull asked Childs whether he thought there was any possibility that Palestinian Arabs could be induced to emigrate to other Arab countries. Childs replied negatively "because of the fundamental attachment of every man to his own homeland." To both Hull and President Roosevelt, the Palestinian question directly involved the interests of the Democratic party. One cynical politician told Childs at the time: "Neither the Democratic nor the Republican Party has the slightest interest in the merits of the Palestine problem. There is no Arab vote in the United States but consider the number of Zionists in New York, a state which can be crucial in a national election."

American policy in the Middle East has been guided by such domestic political considerations since before World War II. On November 1, 1938, an Associated Press dispatch from Jerusalem reported that "a wave of anti-American sentiment swept Arab communities of the Near East today. This feeling was aroused by the action of a large number of governors, senators and representatives, and prominent churchmen, in submitting a memorandum to President Roosevelt urging him to intercede with Great Britain to . . . permit undiminished immigration."

Professional career officers, both at State and in the field, men chiefly concerned with the protection of American interests, were increasingly bypassed on Palestine. Secretary of Defense James Forrestal tells in his *Diaries* how he failed to get leaders of both parties to remove Palestine from domestic politics in order to deal with it solely on the basis of America's foreign interests.

On May 17, 1939, following an inconclusive roundtable of Jews, Arabs, and Britons in London, the British issued a white paper which solemnly declared that it was not British policy to turn Palestine into a Jewish state—nor, for that matter, into an Arab state. Instead, London suggested ending the mandate within ten years, setting up a Palestinian state, possibly with a federal base, and allowing Jewish immigration to rise until it represented one third of the total population (up from 28 percent at the time).

The outbreak of World War II eased United States pressures on the British and Palestine was quickly forgotten as hostilities engulfed the globe. But Zionist leaders, who now felt betrayed by London spent the war years preparing for the coming show-down battle with the British. When peace returned, Hitler's genocide of the Jews and the supercharged emotional atmosphere it engendered made rational thinking about United States interests in the Middle East all but impossible.

The Western world's guilt complex played a decisive role— guilt over the failure to react before the war against Hitler's persecution before it became a "final solution." The subsequent injustice of making room for the Jews in Palestine at the expense of the Palestinians was barely noticed.

On February 24, 1945, at a meeting between Roosevelt and King Ibn Saud at Great Bitter Lake in the Suez Canal, the president pledged America's word that it would not do anything hostile against the Arabs or change its policy without full and prior consultation with both Arabs and Jews. These verbal assurances were confirmed in writing by President Truman to Ibn Saud on April 5, 1945.

Yet shortly before the congressional elections in 1946, Truman endorsed the Jewish Agency's latest proposal for partition and "a viable Jewish state in an adequate area of Palestine" and announced that he was in favor of the immediate admission to Palestine of a hundred thousand Jews. Not to be outdone, Governor Dewey, the Republican party leader, topped his rival by asking "why only 100,000? Why not several hundred thousand Jews?" And the British, completely dependent on United States aid, went along with White House desires which, in turn, were motivated to a large degree by electoral reasons.

When Ibn Saud complained that the United States had already broken a solemn pledge, he explained that what the Arabs were objecting to was not a Jewish enclave on the coast of Palestine, but the creation of a state, which they feared would quickly spread over most of Palestine. Even Palestine itself, the king added, would soon prove insufficient to fulfill the Zionist objective for the great in-gathering.

When the United States came out for partition—i.e., a separate Jewish state—there were numerous reports from United States ambassadors forecasting the consequences of our espousal of the Zionist cause. In brief, they predicted open warfare and the gradual deterioration of our positions in the Arab world.

The United States was jolted, but only briefly, by the storm our action provoked. Secretary of State George C. Marshall talked about "the vital elements in our national security." Ambassadors in the field were given to understand that United States interests, not the exigencies of United States domestic politics, would prevail. Presidential envoy Edwin A. Locke journeyed to Saudi Arabia to convey these assurances personally to the king.

The Arabs expected not United States support for the Arab cause, but simply impartiality. The Americans had been considered traditional friends of the Arab world—as evidenced by the American University at Beirut and the American University at Cairo. But while Locke was on tour, a bitter struggle was developing between United States policy makers and Democratic party strategists. Marshall was overruled; and domestic political concerns prevailed once more.

On March 30, 1948, a special session of the United Nations General Assembly was called, prompted by the United States, to consider the future of Palestine. The rest of the scenario had already been written. The arm-twisting conducted by United States officials, coached by David Niles from the White House, was the toughest ever seen. Under constant pressure from the United States, the British finally announced they would pull out of Palestine May 14, 1948. The Israeli state was proclaimed the same day. War, as predicted, ensued. Some eight hundred thousand Palestinians fled or were forced to flee, evicted as many were from homes and farms by the victorious Israelis.

Israel wound up with all the territory allotted to the Jewish state under United Nations partition plus half the area awarded to the Arabs. The defeated Arabs were left with Samaria, Judea, and the old city of Jerusalem. They felt betrayed by a friend. When Russia recognized Israel hours later, the impact on Arab opinion was negligible. Arabs had never considered the Soviet Union a friend.

The Middle East has been in a state of worsening political and social crisis ever since. Some of the basic facts of the situation have long since been forgotten. Few people seem to realize that for a period of over thirteen hundred years—since the seventh century—Palestinian Arabs enjoyed uninterrupted occupation of the land now known as Israel. And prior to the arrival of Abraham, the Canaanites had it for about two thousand years. In 1918, when the British occupied Palestine, there were fifty-six thousand Jews in the country, representing 8 percent of the total population. Jewish land holdings, 162,500 acres, were 2 percent of the total land area of Palestine.

George Antonius, writing in 1938 about the persecution of the Jews in Nazi Germany before World War II, was clairvoyant when he warned that "to place the brunt of the burden upon Arab Palestine is a miserable evasion of the duty that lies upon the whole of the civilized world. No code of morals can justify the persecution of one people in an attempt to relieve the persecution of another. The cure for the eviction of the Jews from Germany is not to be sought in the eviction of the Arabs from their homeland; and the relief of Jewish distress may not be accomplished at the cost of inflicting corresponding distress upon an innocent and peaceful population."

This is exactly what Britain, coaxed by the United States, allowed to happen ten years later. And now that Israel has conquered Sinai and the West Bank and the Golan plateau, including the Syrian city of Kuneitra, it is hardly surprising that bitterness and fear run deeper than ever. This is not to say that the Arabs are blameless. Far from it. They have repeatedly thrown away opportunities for peace. But alienation and frustration inevitably lead to fantasy and reckless action. The Palestinians—two and a half million of them today—are the new Jews, people who have been wronged by history and persecuted and who argue, with implacable logic, that if the Jews are entitled to their own homeland, all the more reason why they should have one, too. The fact that King Hussein's Bedouins defeated the Palestine guerillas does not really change the problem.

Arnold Toynbee put it this way: "The Jews have an unquestionable right to reside in Judea for religious purposes. Subject to the consent of the Arab inhabitants, they also had a right to buy land . . . from Arab owners and to plant Jewish settlers on purchased land in numbers that would not have threatened to swamp the Arab population. But they had no right to seize by military force the territory that has now become the state of Israel, and to turn its Arab inhabitants into either second-class citizens of Israel, or into refugees whom the Israelis are depriving of their homes and their property."

To understand the depth of Arab feelings, one might ask what kind of reaction would be seen in the United States if the United Nations—with the power to make it stick—were to give away American territory. Toynbee, lecturing at McGill University ten years ago, said, "The Jewish treatment of the Palestinian Arabs in 1947 was as morally indefensible as the slaughter by the Nazis of six million Jews." In *Memories*, the autobiography of Nahum Goldmann, the former president of the world Zionist organization writes that "even Theodor Herzl's brilliantly simple formulation of the Jewish question as basically a transportation problem of 'moving a people without a land into a land without a people' is tinged with disquieting blindness to the Arab claim to Palestine. Palestine was not a land without a people even in Herzl's time; it was inhabited by hundreds of thousands of Arabs who, in the normal course of events, would sooner or later have achieved independent statehood. . . ."

Is Israel an expansionist power? Personally, I do not think so. But Israel is at an impasse in its own actions. Prominent Israeli intellectuals have said so themselves. In a roundtable I conducted for *Newsweek* in Jerusalem (April 7, 1970), the six participants, all dissenters from the official line, agreed that their country was sliding into *de facto* annexation. Professor Michael Bruno called it "creeping annexation . . . the majority of our population is against annexation but present day-to-day policies are likely to lead us into it." Meron Benvenisti, who is the mayor of Jerusalem's deputy for the Arab part of the city, thought "our greatest mistake was to insist on total peace. All or nothing. As a result, some very important decisions, that could have been taken three or four months after the Six-Day War, were turned down by the government." Ben Porath said "the decision to settle 250 Jewish families in Hebron [an Arab town on the West Bank] was a major turning point. Hebron was the first such move since the annexation of Jerusalem when security was not invoked. Historical considerations were given as the reason. Once you embark on such a policy there is no end to it. There is a large body of public opinion and political power in Israel that is very unhappy with the situation and looks for signs in the Arab world that would justify going in another direction. But we should give Arab moderates something to hold on to. A solemn declaration will give them hope of an alternative." Shimon Shamir, the head of the Institute for Middle Eastern Studies at Tel Aviv University, advocated "a solemn government White Paper that would define, for the first time in the history of Zionism, its ultimate goals in this piece of land. It would also recognize the right to nationhood for the Palestinians along borders that will have to be negotiated when the time comes. We should stop new settlements on the West Bank and in Sinai. Allow Palestinians who once lived on the West Bank and are now on the East Bank to return. Why not? If we're not going to annex the West Bank what do we have to fear? Compensation and resettlement of refugees. All these things could clear the air a bit, improve the atmosphere and give arguments to the Palestinians who would be willing to believe us."

Creeping annexation, they all agreed, will leave Israel but two options: either Israel will remain a Jewish but undemocratic state or remain a democratic but not Jewish state. If Israelis want to preserve their Jewish character with what will become an almost half Arab population, Israel will have to deprive the Arabs of their legitimate share of political and government management. Democracy could only be maintained if full rights were given to the Arabs. Which would mean, eventually, the erosion of the Jewish character.

Amos Tversky concluded the roundtable discussion on a pessimistic note. "We'll find a way," he said, "in which Arabs will live in Israel and for various reasons will not participate in political life. Hence Israel will become less democratic as creeping annexation continues. And the Jewish character will be preserved at the price of abandoning an essential part of what the Zionist ideal is all about—which is why we're here in the first place."

Since that time Israel has been trying to maneuver the United States into a position whereby its commitment to defend Israel, as it existed prior to the 1967 war, becomes extended, *de facto,* to include the occupied territories. Both President Nixon and Secretary Rogers are acutely aware of the danger of confrontation with the Soviets if this is allowed to happen and it is for this reason that they have called for Israeli withdrawal to the 1967 borders—with "minor adjustments."

Nixon owes less to Jewish voters than any president since World War II. He came to office convinced that the time had come for a more evenhanded policy in the Mideast. Yet Nixon has still not managed to steer the United States to a new course. After Israel walked out of the Jarring talks in 1970, because they said the Egyptians had violated the standstill agreement by inserting more Soviet missiles in the canal zone, Jerusalem managed to extract $500 million worth of United States military hardware from Washington as its price for returning to the United Nations mediator's office. There was no commitment to evacuate the occupied territories.

Evidence that the Israeli lobby is still a major factor in United States politics was seen when sophisticated political leaders like John Lindsay and Nelson Rockefeller, men of national stature, felt compelled to deliver calculated diplomatic insults to foreign leaders who do not agree with Israel's present policy.

Israel has managed to convince many gullible congressmen and Pentagon officials that it is a bastion of Western democracy in a sea of Soviet client states. Israelis generated scare headlines when the Soviets began installing SAM-3 missiles (defensive weapons with a range of fourteen miles) in Egypt and later sent up their own pilots on air defense missions. (The Soviets, incidentally, lost five of their own pilots in a single dogfight over Egypt.) The Russians had, in effect, accepted complete responsibility for Egypt's anti-aircraft defenses. But overlooked in all the brouhaha was the fact that Israel had left the Egyptians and the Russians no alternative. Israel's deep penetration raids into the Egyptian heartland had so humiliated Nasser that he made a secret dash to Moscow to get the Russians to bail him out. Some third country experts in the Mideast are convinced that the Israelis did not overplay their military hand, which was a fashionable line of speculation at the time, but wanted all this to happen for the sake of polarizing the conflict between East and West.

With an independent United States Mideast policy, the situation would not have deteriorated to the extent that it has since the Six-Day War. After his defeat, Nasser was ready to accept Israel in its pre-war frontiers. But the United States allowed Israeli positions to harden. No one bothered holding the Israelis to all the heady talk I heard from high officials right after the war about "surprising the Arabs with our generosity and magnanimity." Meanwhile, Soviet influence has steadily deepened.

To Moscow's delight, we have allowed the Middle East to become a simple equation of East vs. West. Russia has large chunks of the Arab world under its influence and we have Israel upholding the banner of the free world. In terms of principles, it may be beautiful, but in terms of geopolitics it doesn't make much sense. "It is manifestly absurd," *The Economist* wrote recently, "that a large collection of countries, just across the Mediterranean from Europe, should grow steadily more hostile to Western interests for no other reason than their belief that the entire Western world gives unqualified support for Israel."

Russia's main interest, Israeli officials argue privately, is in reopening the Suez Canal so that it can link up the various component parts of its new global naval strategy—Black Sea, Mediterranean, Red Sea, Persian Gulf, and Indian Ocean—and pose a mortal threat to Europe's and Japan's oil jugular in the Gulf. Ergo, we should help them stay where they are and keep the canal closed. The argument impresses armchair strategists whose powers of reasoning and deduction leave something to be desired.

The Russians now have about fifty ships on station in the Mediterranean and another twenty in the Indian Ocean (which operate out of Pacific coast bases or come round the Cape of

Good Hope). The Soviets are very active in Iran, Iraq, and Kuwait, all three Persian Gulf powers, and their ships occasionally sail up the Gulf to Basra in Iraq. They do all this without the Suez Canal. So reopening the canal, while convenient but certainly not essential to the Soviets, would be more than just convenient to the West European powers, America's closest allies. At a time of rapidly rising oil prices, the shorter trip through the canal would be a tremendous boon to Europe's economies; the recently negotiated 30 percent increase in oil prices would be partially compensated by a 20 percent drop in freight charges.

If the Soviet Union has become the dominant foreign influence in the Middle East, inept United States diplomacy, hamstrung by political pressures at home, is chiefly to blame. In a few short years, we have seen Soviet proxies establish themselves in Egypt, Syria, Iraq, North Yemen, South Yemen, Somalia, Algeria, Libya, and the Sudan. Libya may be anti-Communist but it is now buying most of its army hardware from Russia while the Sudan executed its leading Communists but kept some fifteen hundred advisers from Communist countries. If similar proxies manage to establish themselves astride the oil resources of the Gulf, all the Western European countries, as well as Japan, may find themselves doing more business with Moscow than their vital interests would allow. Coupled with West Germany's Ostpolitik and Moscow's drive for a European security conference, it does not require too much effort of imagination to perceive how Soviet influence in the Persian Gulf could lead to the gradual Finlandization of Western Europe— and a drastic shift in the world balance of power against the United States.

Peter the Great (1682-1725) and Catherine the Great (1762-1796) already had visions of a Russian empire extending southward through the Mediterranean into the Middle East but it was not until the mid-1950s that Russia succeeded in breaking down traditional Western influence in the area. Russia has inherited America's old mantle as the champion of Arab nationalism. America has lost most of its once tremendously powerful influence in the Arab world. We are the despised traitor who sanctions Israeli expansion. Yet Egyptian leaders still concede privately that only the United States, not the Soviet Union, can exert the kind of pressure that will restore peace in the

Middle East, as well as the balance of geopolitical power. They would welcome such a change as they do not relish the prospect of an ever-closer relationship with Moscow.

By persuading Israel to go back to its 1967 boundaries (with a few minor rectifications), or at least accepting the 1967 frontiers as a basis for negotiation, in return for a peace treaty guaranteed by the powers, the United States could go a long way in halting the drift toward complete Soviet domination of the Middle East. Until that happens, Russia will be Egypt's only guarantee against further Israeli encroachment.

Moscow's Middle Eastern campaign is not ideologically motivated. It is a classic geopolitical power play. The Russians have a practical interest in Arab oil—not to deny it to West Europe and Japan, but to control it and acquire an increasingly large share of it themselves. It should be recalled that in 1947 Moscow demanded Iranian oil concessions as a condition for pulling out its forces from Azerbaijan.

It has usually been assumed that Russia had more than enough oil to satisfy domestic demand. But by 1980, if not before, production will fall short of consumption. Moreover, East Europe's requirements, over half of which are now supplied by Moscow, will triple by the end of the decade. So Moscow's growing interest in Middle Eastern oil is also motivated by the imperative desire to retain its domination over Eastern Europe.

Egypt's need for modern weaponry in the mid-fifties, to consolidate the power of Nasser's revolution and his leadership of the Arab world, was Russia's opening wedge. United States foreign policy was then run by a man who suffered from "pactomania," mesmerized as he was by military alliances against the Soviet Union, and who rejected neutralism as an evil heresy. Nasser's request for no-strings military hardware was turned down and Russia obtained a virtually free geopolitical ride into the Middle East. The Soviet Union nimbly leapfrogged over the West's elaborate collective defense arrangements against Russian expansion. Washington had failed to see that neutrality and independence and modern Arab nationalism were all synonymous. This lesson was learned, belatedly, in 1958 when Camille Chamoun, Lebanon's pro-Western president, was forced out of power for aligning his country with the Western bloc in return for United States aid.

It is crucial to remember, however, that Israel began getting arms from France a year before Egypt received any from the Soviet bloc. In 1954, France, obsessed with the suspicion that Cairo was responsible for the nationalist rebellions in North Africa, agreed to help Israel launch a major rearmament program.

Nasser made his first guns-for-cotton deal with the Soviet bloc a year later, in September 1955, but all was not yet lost for the United States. The Egyptian leader's most ambitious scheme was the new high dam on the Nile above Aswan, designed to triple Egypt's arable land and provide power for new industries. The United States, Britain, and the World Bank had offered $268 million to finance this key project for Egypt's future, mainly to forestall a Soviet offer. By mid-1956, negotiations were well advanced. But the Zionist lobby, with an assist from the still powerful Chinese Nationalist lobby, which was incensed by Nasser's recognition of Communist China, was hard at work to scuttle the Aswan negotiations. I was foreign editor of *Newsweek* at the time and remember well the visits I received from Israeli diplomats and Americans lobbying for Taiwan, trying to convince me that Egypt had already become a Soviet satellite and that the Aswan deal, if it went through, would be tantamount to promoting our own demise in the Middle East.

John Foster Dulles presumably came to the conclusion that Congress would not sanction a United States contribution and, on July 19, 1956, with a diplomatic slap in the face that was heard around the world, canceled the deal as precipitously as it was made six months earlier. Nasser could not leave such an insult unanswered. A week later he nationalized the Suez Canal. Moscow moved into the Aswan picture with a flourish, eventually lending Cairo $554 million of the $800 million-plus cost.

But for a very foolish decision, probably the second most costly foreign policy mistake of the post-war era (only Vietnam was costlier), Richard Nixon, not Russian President Podgorny, would have been feted at Aswan for the big inauguration in January 1970. More important, both the 1956 and 1967 Arab-Israeli wars could have been avoided, too.

Instead, the world was treated to a disgraceful, collusive plot between France, Britain, and Israel to overthrow Nasser by force of arms. Losing their cool, France and Britain charged

Cairo with piracy and aggression. An invasion force was assembled in the Mediterranean while Dulles tried to promote compromise. London and Paris said Egypt was totally unfit to run the canal on its own—which was soon disproved as traffic rose to record levels under Egyptian management.

Under pressure from the United Nations Secretary-General Dag Hammarskjold, Nasser finally conceded that the American-proposed Suez Canal Users' Association should collect the tolls from all the maritime nations and allocate the revenue to the new Egyptian Canal Authority to be used for the canal's operating costs and development. France, by then convinced that Algeria's war of independence would collapse without Nasser's support, rejected the eminently reasonable compromise and determined to have a showdown with Cairo.

French and Israeli officials secretly concocted the Suez invasion scenario: 1) Israel would invade Sinai; 2) France and Britain would invade the canal zone under the pretext of protecting the waterway; 3) Nasser would fall, or if he didn't, the invasion force would push through to Cairo and overthrow the regime. Britain, in an act of political madness, went along with the crackbrained scheme and even added a new wrinkle to the plot: Britain and France would issue an ultimatum to both sides to pull back, which they knew Egypt would reject, and then would intervene, supposedly to separate the combatants (and at the same time reoccupy the canal).

The French and the British had manufactured war out of the nationalization of the Suez Canal and the Arabs understandably became convinced that the imperialist powers were backing an attempt to recolonize the Arab world. The French supplied Israel with forty-five French Air Force fighter-bombers and pilots for the invasion, in addition to the one hundred previously delivered under the arms deal.

The United States momentarily recovered prestige in the Arab world when it put its full weight behind the United Nations to force withdrawal of the Franco-British expeditionary force and the Israeli army. But this was quickly negated by the Eisenhower Doctrine which was seen as an attempt to enlist the Arabs in an anti-Soviet crusade in return for aid. Nasser, meanwhile, whose prestige had soared to new heights as a result of his "victory" against the combined forces of Britain, France, and

Israel, told the Arabs to refuse aid that was linked to any form of obligation to fight the West's battles.

There were few subscribers to the doctrine. International communism did not greatly worry the Arabs. Israel did. Many prominent Americans already were confusing Nasserism and communism and it was not too hard for Moscow to convince the Arabs that the Eisenhower Doctrine was directed against Arab nationalism. Moscow became firmly entrenched as a champion of the Arab cause.

After the United Arab Republic union with Syria on February 1, 1958, and Abdul Karim Kassem's coup that toppled Iraq's monarchy, Nasser seemed unassailable. But he rapidly overplayed his hand, fomenting civil war in Lebanon and plotting an army coup against King Hussein in Jordan. It was only the last minute intervention of United States Marines in Lebanon and British paratroops in Jordan—a sort of last hurrah for Western gunboat diplomacy—that prevented revolutionary takeovers in both countries.

Yet despite all his subsequent setbacks, Nasser retained tremendous influence and prestige. For 80 million Arabs, he remained the paramount leader and the prophet of the revolution until he drew his last breath trying to negotiate an end to Jordan's civil war of September 1970.

President Kennedy's attempt to forge a new set of relations with Nasser, as the acknowledged leader of the Arab world, came to a pitiable end when the Johnson Administration cut off massive quantities of food that had been sent under the New Frontier's "Food for Peace" (PL480) program. It was Aswan all over again. An impatient United States government, prodded by the Israeli lobby, felt Nasser was too overly engaged in playing America off against Russia. But stopping the food, on which Egypt had become heavily dependent, did the United States more harm, long term, than if the aid had never been given in the first place.

The fact that the United States had invested more in Egypt ($1.2 billion between 1954 and 1965) than the Soviet Union ($1 billion during the same period) had once again become irrelevant. The United States had opposed Nasser and occasionally sided with him but nearly always in a manner unrelated to its interests.

From the opening days of the Kennedy administration through the Johnson and Nixon administrations, Nasser, in private conversations, was puzzled at the way our moves seemed divorced from the objective of making gains. He used to insist that a political analyst visiting Earth from Mars, and examining American moves in the Middle East solely according to criteria of self-interest, would be similarly puzzled.

Regardless of disappointments and difficulties, Russia, by contrast, showed infinite patience. Moscow suffered many setbacks and calculated insults but never lost sight of the long-term objective. Israel's victory in 1967 was a crushing blow to Russia's prestige—as the Arabs' main protector and purveyor of arms. But Moscow astutely, in my judgment, opted for massive resupply rather than disengagement and today Arab dependency on the Soviet Union is greater than ever.

Israel's new "strategic frontiers" and what appears to many Arabs as an expansionist policy has also been a great asset to Russia in reestablishing its paramountcy. The Soviet-Egyptian treaty concluded in the summer of 1971 doubtless outweighs, in Moscow's judgment, the embarrassment of the trial of pro-Soviet Egyptian ministers who tried to overthrow Sadat.

Dealing with the Arabs requires a great deal of patience and understanding, two commodities that always seem to be in short supply in Washington. The volcanic condition of the Middle East, Anthony Nutting wrote in his book *The Arabs,* is partly due to the fact that the Arabs, like probably no other people in the world except the Irish, "are irrational and emotional to a point where they think only with their hearts, never with their heads. . . . They are . . . incapable of seeing people or issues in any shade between jet-black and snow-white. No Arab will ever forget a gesture of friendship; likewise he will always remember an act of hostility. No race on earth will more eagerly or cheerfully cut off its nose to spite its face. If their dignity is offended or their trust betrayed, the Arabs will react or retaliate without thought of the consequences . . . not even the likely interests of the Arab community can be used with any certainty as a barometer of Arab reaction."

What about United States policy in the Middle East in the years to come? Even after the establishment of Israel, and the Arab defeat of 1949, the United States still enjoyed some credit and prestige because those were the halcyon days when America was in the vanguard of decolonization and social and economic reform. Our secret operatives worked fairly closely with Nasser's Free Officers Committee while it was plotting King Farouk's downfall. But in the mid-fifties domestic considerations returned to the fore. First there was Israel—and the Israeli lobby. But, second, there was also oil. This, in turn, led to hostility for the emerging forces of "progressive" Pan-Arab nationalism, which stood for cooperative socialism and a redistribution of wealth, and to a certain fondness of the *ancien régime,* the feudal rulers who knew how to suppress communism and support such still-born defense arrangements as the Baghdad Pact, in return for fabulous oil royalties and other forms of aid.

One of our principal mistakes was to lose our nerve with Nasser and say, in effect, let the other side have him. We comforted ourselves with the notion that the countries that really mattered in the Arab world were safe—Saudi Arabia, Kuwait, Libya, the Persian Gulf states, all the big oil producers with the exception of Iraq. Libya was constantly cited to me by Israeli diplomats as an example of how United States support for Israel does not necessarily drive America out of the Arab world. Libya, among the world's three principal oil exporting nations, is now a frontrunner in the Socialist revolutionary camp—and has exploded a few more myths along the way.

It is not too late for the United States to recoup its losses in the Middle East and restore some balance with the Soviet Union —and perhaps help prevent yet another round of fighting between Arabs and Israelis. Egypt's dependence on the Soviet Union, while extensive, should not be exaggerated. Egypt is neither puppet nor satellite, but client state. There is little affection for the patronizing Russians in the Arab world. Soviet military advisers treat their wards with contempt. Western tourists are greeted like long-lost friends while Eastern tourists, still the majority in Egypt, are regarded with the cold disdain a head-waiter might show for a diner who undertips.

I have spoken with several Egyptians who live in apartment buildings that also house Russian families. There is never any contact, except the occasional nod and greeting as they share the same elevator. The thinking element in Egypt is still almost entirely Western-oriented—from their reading habits to their consumer preferences. Eastern goods are the butt of endless jokes.

Promises of rapid economic growth under Soviet-style planned economies have proved hollow, and free enterprise has made rapid strides since Sadat took over.

The degree of Soviet control is the subject of much debate. There is still no definitive answer to this crucial question. In 1967, things clearly got out of hand, not because the Soviets couldn't rein in Nasser, but because the Israelis went to war. Everyone miscalculated, including, incidentally, the Israelis who thought their tremendous victory would bring the Arabs to their knees and make them sue for peace.

If there is no agreement by Israel to withdraw, as suggested by none other than Ben-Gurion himself, can the Russians force the Egyptians to continue to hold their fire? This, too, remains to be seen. The alternative could be another shattering defeat for Russia's most sophisticated military hardware. Would Moscow stand idly by once again? I personally doubt it. For openers, Moscow might decide to throw its own MIG squadrons into the air battle, with, of course, the attendant risk of rapid escalation into another Cuban-type confrontation with the United States.

When forty United States senators show up to hear Abba Eban, the Israeli foreign minister, and only six to listen to William Rogers, the American secretary of state, before the Senate Foreign Relations Committee, one realizes the distance that remains to a more evenhanded United States policy in the Mideast. And when one hears responsible senators denounce an international peacekeeping force, including units of the Big Four powers, as a betrayal tantamount to turning Israel over to Russia's not-too-tender mercies, one despairs of ever finding a way out.

There has never been any thought of putting Soviet troops on Israel's borders. A joint Soviet-American peacekeeping force was first suggested in a *Washington Post* editorial in August 1970. The idea was to station American troops on Israel's 1967 frontier with Egypt and Russian troops on the western banks of the canal with a demilitarized Sinai desert in between. The presence of Soviet units in the mix was designed to reassure Egypt and the presence of United States units was to do the same for Israel. The Russians would not be any closer to Israel than they already are today.

Senator Henry Jackson says such a scheme would legalize the Soviet presence in the Mideast. It is already perfectly legal today. There is no way of getting the Russians out as part of a package deal, as suggested by the senator from Washington. But there is a way of balancing their presence. Once the United States has prevailed upon Israel to pull back, American diplomacy will recover its freedom to maneuver in countries that are now Soviet client states.

Israel says all international guarantees have proved worthless in the past. Quite true. But the powers are now discussing something quite different—guarantees that would be linked to the Security Council where each of the Big Four has a veto. Israel refuses to acknowledge the difference.

The Rogers Plan, the United States peace initiative, recent statements by Nixon and Rogers, are all steps in the right direction. But they are not sufficient. Israel has not budged and the only way to provoke real movement is to make future aid to Israel conditional on withdrawal in return for a formal peace treaty.

Whether Israel likes it or not, Russia and America will have to work together to keep the peace and we can work toward the same objective without formal cooperation, which still seems precluded by the ideological great divide. By involving the Soviet Union in international peacekeeping, we may also help inhibit its systematic policy of undermining United States and other Western interests—e.g., in the Gulf. The Israeli issue will no longer be the most convenient way of doing this.

I have never subscribed to the theory that Moscow sought chaos or permanent war in the Middle East. It wanted, and still wants, the kind of stable Arab regimes it can deal with, as safe from right wing coups as from left wing radical influence. A resumption of fighting along the canal—inevitable unless Israel agrees to withdraw—can only bring more humiliations to the Arabs—and the risk of involving the Soviet Union in a larger conflict.

The alternative to some form of cooperation with the United States in the search for a lasting settlement, which Egypt now wants, would be for Russia to begin supporting the more extremist positions of Libya's Colonel Khadaffi, such as the demand for the overthrow of all moderate governments, the radicalization of the Arab world and the destruction of the Israeli state. Moscow knows it can no longer continue to be all things to all Arabs.

To make sure that a peaceful settlement would be a lasting one, however, an additional, strictly United States guarantee, as suggested by Senator Fulbright last year, would seem to be in order. In the wake of the United Nation's dismal record in the Mideast and America's failures in Vietnam, there is a legitimate doubt in Israel about American intentions if a combination of Soviet power and Arab subversion were gnawing away at the foundations of the Jewish state. A formal treaty, ratified by the Senate, under which the United States would guarantee "the territory and independence of Israel within the 1967 borders" would, as Ben-Gurion put it, constitute better security than the continued occupation of Arab lands.

After Israel's frontiers come the Palestinian refugees—and the gut issue of a Palestinian state. The Arab-Israeli conflict is more accurately described as the War of the Palestinian Succession. Israel and Jordan are the two successor states of Britain's Palestine Mandate and King Hussein and his three hundred thousand Bedouin supporters have become an anachronism in a country that has a predominantly Palestinian population. In addition to adequate financial compensation, the refugees would have to be given a voice in a referendum to decide whether they want to remain a semi-autonomous part of Jordan, on the west bank, or have their own sovereign state. If the latter, the new Palestinian state would presumably incorporate all of Jordan, both east and west bank, as there does not seem to be room for a third state between Iraq and the Mediterranean. Even pre-1967 Jordan was of dubious viability. The west bank alone, whether or not linked to a free port on Israel's Mediterranean coast, would either be an Israeli puppet, which Palestinian leaders could not accept, or a radical Palestinian state, run along Cuban lines, which Israel could not accept.

The crux of the problem is how to insert Israel into the Arab world where it belongs, not as a Western enclave but as a progressive Middle Eastern state. For that Israel must help promote the creation of a Palestinian entity with which, long-term, it could confederate, a sort of Austro-Hungarian empire made up of Jews and Palestinians, two of the world's most intelligent races. There is no reason why this new complex could not declare its neutrality in the geopolitical contest between East and West. And the United States could help promote this evolution by demonstrating that United States and Israeli interests do not necessarily coincide. Eventually, this confederal Palestinian state would become the interlocutor for other Arab countries. Now that the extremist leadership of the Palestinian movement is discredited by the rank-and-file after a long series of military and political and diplomatic blunders, there is an opportunity to tackle the Palestinian problem anew. It cannot be ignored because it will always have the potential to wreck the peace. In my opinion, there is no lasting settlement in the Middle East without a Palestinian state. The solution to the hardest problem of all—Israel's annexation of East Jerusalem— is discernible in this context.

Only after a just peace has been restored on a more equitable basis can the United States hope to contribute to the stability of the area by promoting regional development programs (e.g., a common market). Oil revenue will peter out in approximately three decades—the same time that has elapsed since 1940. There is much to be done if the Arab world is to prosper without the black gold at the end of this period. Arab nationalism, now a major force for instability in the Mideast, must be harnessed to the problems of development—as European nationalism is today. United States technology is essential to success and the Arabs recognize it.

Another round of fighting will only make matters worse. The Six-Day War already added two hundred thousand new Palestinian refugees to the million already living around the perimeter of Israel. Nor can the United States opt out of the picture. If we did so, the effect on our NATO allies in the Mediterranean is easy to imagine. The defense of Western Europe itself would be in question. As a matter of high national policy, the United States must press for change in the Middle East and once again take its place in the vanguard of progress. The status quo can only lead to more chaos.

United States Policy and Latin American Politics: from Alliance For Progress to Action For Progress

Irving Louis Horowitz

DAG HAMMERSKJOLD KEPT a diary which was later published as *Markings;* I am sorely tempted to call this presentation: "mutterings." My observations come to you without footnotes and without the anxiety-relieving formal apparatus of scholarship. In fact, this paper is as tight as a bowl of Jello left in the sunshine for an hour. On the other hand, the topic, "United States Policy Toward Latin America," does not exactly permit a rigorous, formal approach. I am impressed by the fact that despite the erstwhile efforts of major journals such as *Foreign Affairs* and *Foreign Policy,* there is still an obvious need for mutterings dignified as an overview.

The theme of United States policy toward Latin America has been discussed and examined in most governmental and academic circles with the assumption that there is in fact an entity called United States Policy in Latin America. Regretfully, I must declare that the theme of my paper is to deny the very premise of its title. I find slender evidence to support the thesis that there is an entity called United States Policy in or Toward or About Latin America. This is not to deny that there have been a series of major decisions which have drastically and at times dramatically affected affairs in Latin America. But such policy decisions do not flow from an overall grand design, and certainly do not emanate from any hemispheric posture.

What does one do with conflicting interpretations of the same events? How does one measure such factors as dependence and independence, investment made from altruistic motives and investment based on egoistic motives? The analyst of United States foreign policy is faced with the problem of two cultures: one is structural analysis which places the blame for Latin American underdevelopment squarely on the external variable called imperialism; the other model is based upon an analysis which places the blame for underdevelopment on internal variables—such as religion, traditionalism, climate, race, etc. Nor does it suffice to say that the truth is some admixture of the two—since this form of question begging does not come to terms with the existence of special problems affecting Latin American relations with the United States. If imperialism is ubiquitous, why is there such a differential response, country by country? If cultural and sociological factors like race and religion are so powerful, why does there seem to be such a strong connection between the problems of Latin America as a whole and the penetration of United States capital?

The answers given seem to be a function of the interests of the examiner more than intrinsic to the nature of what is being examined. Nonetheless, we are obligated to assess these competing claims of hemispheres and empires.

The issues generated by United States foreign policy in and toward Latin America are of a magnitude calculated to increase frustration and ferocity, but hardly reason or relaxation. For one economist, the United States is simply the center of an imperial domain under growing pressure by the international monopolies to formulate and implement political and economic policies which will create an attractive investment climate in Latin America and the Third World. Economic development is thus promoted by the United States as a means for anxiously seeking outlets for its economic surplus. For another economist, the United States effort to aid development is one of the noblest experiments in selfless giving—an attempt to help create enough stability to ward off the thrusts of totalitarianism. Thus, foreign aid as an instrument of United States foreign policy is the most mature expression of the American corporate belief in itself—in capitalism.

United States foreign policy toward Latin America is not only often filtered through a grid of Soviet and Chinese aspirations, but also often shaped by entrepreneurial aspirations within the United States government. What occurs is a conflict at the level of policy-making between military sectors who believe in the need to respond always and everywhere to socialist and communist menaces; State Department sectors which tend to advocate a benign approach based upon tolerance and respect for sovereignties as long as business interests are not menaced; and Department of Defense orientations which view intervention as a subtle matter based on generating civic action and counterinsurgency programs. In short, the complexities of the world order make the various formulators of United States policy toward Latin America either substantially or downright self-contradictory.

I.   Ideological Roots of United States Policy

From whence derives the idea of a United States policy in Latin America? The answer is as strikingly clear as it is dramatically underplayed: such an idea derives from an ideological inflexibility and a rhetorical consistency that throughout twentieth century United States history has reflected a profound separation from the realities of policy decisions. As inconsistent and incongruous as our actual policy toward the hemisphere has been, to that very extent our ideology and rhetoric have fostered the idea of a consistent and congruous posture. The beginning of all wisdom about United States policy for the hemisphere is an awareness of the schism between action and doctrine—a schism that becomes exceedingly dangerous to both North Americans and Latin Americans precisely at that point when it is forgotten that foreign policy serves national interests; and that, in fact, whatever moral imperatives exist derive precisely from such highly selective interests.

American foreign policy is often dignified by the term "pragmatism." Its defenders speak of pragmatism as the equivalent of a semisecret operational code book intended to disguise imperialist aggression. But either as a pedestrian or as a sophisticated concept, the claims to a pragmatic foreign policy collapse under the weight of scrutiny. First of all, how can pragmatism serve as a doctrine of imperialism when of its three chief American advocates, William James was the vigorous founder and sponsor of the anti-imperialist league opposing United States intervention in Cuba and the Phillippines; John Dewey was perhaps the most traditionalist opponent of United States involvement in European affairs, arguing that the curse of the world is European machinations, and claiming that even membership in the League of Nations would be untenable and unjustifiable; and Charles Sanders Peirce, who can be accused of many sins, but not imperialism, was the least political of men —at least in the larger sense of politics.

The phrase "pragmatism" is used by American foreign policymakers to indicate a simple doctrine of expedience, of doing what is ostensibly best for the survival of the United States— not a particularly explicit or meaningful foundation for policy. Indeed, an ideological *rigor mortis* has combined with a functional and tactical immaturity to produce a certain crudity in American foreign policy. How could the situation have been otherwise? The United States is a society that did not choose pluralism, but dignified its plethora of doctrines after the fact. Unlike the Soviet Union, or socialist states in general, the capacity of the American system to generate a foreign policy of any consistency is limited. And it is these limitations rather than policies that are consecrated with the word "pragmatism." Whether consistency is a virtue or not is beside the point; rather the point is that pragmatism has been used not as a doctrine or an ideology, but a device revealing the absence of either.

Understanding what is known as United States foreign policy is complicated not only by the emergence of the Third World as an independent force, but by the murkiness of motives and the decision-making itself. For example, to what degree is United States foreign policy shaped by fear of the loss of its $16 billion in corporate assets throughout the Third World, and to what extent by fear of Soviet Communist militancy? In the case of Latin America at least, the preponderant evidence would suggest that the investment portfolio is dominant. Further, the behavior of the Soviet Union has been either revisionist or counterrevolutionist, and therefore the "threat of Communism" either muted or blunted. Ironically, the requirements of its own foreign policy have compelled the Soviet Union to pursue a conservative approach serving as a major brake on radical social change. But the Chinese Communist movement has stepped into this void and has radicalized Latin American Communist behavior in countries such as Brazil, Uruguay, and Chile.

The presumed beaconlight of United States policy toward Latin America has been anti-communism. At the Tenth Inter-

American Conference which met at Caracas in March 1954, the United States intervention into Guatemalan affairs was anticipated on the basis of forging "a clear cut and unmistakable policy determination against the intervention of international communism in the hemisphere." Congress later ratified intervention in the case of Guatemala on the grounds of "the existence of strong evidence of intervention by the international communist movement in the state of Guatemala." Somewhat later, in August 1960, at the foreign ministers' meeting of the Organization of American States at San Jose, it was noted that "all members of the regional organization are under obligation to submit to the discipline of the Inter-American system." And in January 1962 at the Punte del Este meetings of the OAS, this discipline was spelled out: "The adherence by any member of the Organization of American States to Marxism-Leninism is incompatible with the Inter-American system and the alignment of such a government with the communist bloc breaks the unity and solidarity of the hemisphere." The assertion of such broad ranging jurisdictional rights thereby provided the rationale for unqualified intervention into the affairs of the Cuban nation, just as it had eight years earlier in Guatemalan affairs, albeit with far different consequences.

Despite the seeming ideological consistency of United States hemispheric policy, the diversity of Latin American politics created serious problems at the policy level: Cuba became the first socialist regime in the hemisphere, Peru and Bolivia have now declared strong nationalist aims counter to United States policy, while the recent elections which brought Salvador Allende to power make Chile the second avowed socialist regime in the Western hemisphere. The smashing force of political pluralization has struck the hemisphere. The United States response has been to attempt to adjust realities to its ideological posture, which in part, at least, accounts for American advocacy of interventionist policies. But it is extremely doubtful that the same sort of interventionist maneuvers can be maintained in this decade.

United States foreign policy with respect to Latin America is and has been adjudicative at the ideological level, but it has managed to be relatively accommodating at the institutional level. In Mexico, Guatemala, Cuba, the Dominican Republic, and Brazil, where efforts to end colonialism and institutionalize nationalism took place, the United States applied economic sanctions and military intervention in defense of corporate interests.

Latin American policies toward the United States have accommodated this dangerous polarity in United States policy-making. Mexico is a bourgeois one-party state, relatively friendly but clearly nationalistic. Cuba is a peasant proletariat one-party state, flatly hostile to the United States, nationalistic, anti-imperialistic, and friendly to the Soviet Union. Chile represents a socialist front coalition, nationalistic, anti-imperialistic, but maintaining strict neutrality with respect to the Cold War. Chile shows a national policy rather than a hemispheric policy toward problems of socialist development. It has been careful to distinguish its pro-socialist orientation from any anti-American statement. Argentina under Juan Peron was a coalition between middle echelon officer corps, trade-unionist and *déclassé* elements. It was nationalistic, but quite ready to cooperate with the imperial powers of Europe and America by playing them off against each other. In general, then, Latin Americans recently have carefully avoided offending North American ideological sensibilities, but have nonetheless gone about their business without much thought to United States views.

II. Foreign Aid and Foreign Policy: Myths and Realities

Confusion between foreign policy and foreign aid is also rampant. The United States does engage in heavy dosages of foreign aid—at both the civilian and military levels. But whether such aid adds up to a foreign policy is something else again. Foreign aid has been designed to serve many and diverse purposes of United States interests. In the 1940s its primary purpose was European recovery along capitalist and democratic lines. In the 1950s foreign aid was meant to serve the purposes of mutual security; this was the period during which most aid and trade pacts were negotiated with Latin American countries. In the 1960s foreign aid was tied to the tasks of economic development, specifically to making the UN Development Decade successful, and in Latin America this meant underwriting certain activities in the public sector, such as the Alliance for Progress, to act as a countervailing force to private sector imperialism. In the 1970s aid programs are increasingly being linked to an improved human and physical environment. It is probably correct to say that foreign aid in each period was more often spent to satisfy the desires of what is euphemistically termed the cosmopolitan center of the client nations than to advance the interests of their colonized peripheries.

Justification and rationalization of foreign aid differs in each period. In the forties, aid was to create a world safe for capitalism. In the fifties, it was a world safe for democracy, or at least safe from Soviet expansionism. In the sixties, foreign aid was justified primarily as a tool to narrow the gap between wealth and poverty, or, as the geographers say, to broaden the wealth band in the temperate zones surrounded on each side by a wide mass of impoverishment. And as the seventies unfold, it is clear that the orientation is toward problem programs rather than national areas. For example, more attention is being directed to problems of demography and urban explosion than to overseas nations as a whole. These shifts in emphasis have all been responses to national situations, not part of an overall grand plan to deepen the penetration of overseas holdings. In fact, so little federal programming is directed toward specific private sector needs in foreign lands that one must wonder whether the tasks of managing overseas holdings have not been given over, once again, to the North American corporate sector.

The Nixon program of Action for Progress for Latin America follows closely the recommendations of the Rockefeller Commission of 1970. Basically, this report of the commission argues that business and private investment funds are once more to become the main instrument for promoting development. After $20 billion and an Alliance for Progress program that failed to alter any fundamental relationships, Washington is turning once more to private rather than public sector solutions. However, as the Special Latin American Coordinating Commission (CECLA) made clear in its Vina del Mar meetings of 1970, the problem is neither private nor public funding, and therefore the solution is something else again. In fact, listing what CECLA holds to be the main problems makes clear that the tactic of emphasizing private sector over public sector investment simply is wide of the mark. Among the major obstacles blocking Latin American efforts to carry out a coherent, progressive series of reforms in economic and trade relations with the United States, CECLA lists the following: restrictions which seal off equitable or favorable access for Latin American exports to other world markets; the continuing deterioration of the volume, conditions, and means of international financial assistance, aggravated by the need to repay high interest charges on existing debts; imposed difficulties which impede the transfer of technology to the nations of Latin America, thus delaying the modernization of its research and development facilities; the discouragement of multinational trade and aid pacts that would break the cycle of dependence inculcated by bilateral pacts. In many ways, the United States government has avoided dealing with these and other obstacles by going backward rather than forward; that is to say, by putting the entire matter of foreign aid back in the hands of entrepreneurs doing business in Latin America. The United States has abdicated what little policy leverage it once had (which was precious little indeed), and is returning the hemisphere to the source of its ills, private investors, rather than address itself to the cure of such ills.

The matter of perception and perspective is crucial. The United States has rarely had any but a distorted sense not only of its international priorities (witness Southeast Asia) but also of the extent of Latin American nationalism. Not even the Castro revolution seems to have shaken the American faith that Latin American nations are merely an additional twenty states which, added to the fifty already in existence, make a greater United States of seventy states. To be sure, Latin Americans speak Spanish, and they are not as natty and neat as Protestants up North; but, that notwithstanding, the Latin American nations have come to be treated as states. Lyndon B. Johnson, in particular, tended to put his arm around Latin American presidents as if they were governors, with appropriate and respectful knee slapping, before the inevitable question: what can I do for you today? It was as if dignitaries of Ecuador or Mexico are simply state representatives sent from the folks back home with petty squabbles needing arbitration.

There is a vocabulary of motives that divides Latin America from the United States that no amount of revision in foreign policy on either side can or will remove. What for the United States is the containment of communism is for most Latin American governments pure and simple intervention. What the United States sees as dangerous tendencies toward socialism as a result of expropriation may for Latin Americans simply be a half-way house of nationalization of basic industry. What the United States sees as assistance Latins see as containment or even intervention. Thus, the vocabulary of motive imprints its diachronic series of words upon the facts, causing an escalation of rhetoric and response far beyond the actual problems which may exist. There is further a complication over what Latin Americans want: the products and results of development or the control of the actual process for gaining development. More simply: do Latin Americans want a first rate set of pots and pans made in the United States, or do they want a second rate set that are of domestic manufacture? Is national production or national pride the key to their attitudes, and hence the basis of their foreign policy posture?

My feeling is that such questions are beyond the scope of survey research techniques. For what is involved are decisions that may work equally well or equally poorly, but with different consequences for different social classes and interest groups. Any powerful nation, whatever its motivations, will be hard put to convince the recipients of aid or trade of the special nobility that permits one nation to be in a superordinate role, while twenty nations remain in a subordinate role. There is a sense in which the fundamentals of social psychology, rather than the fundamentals of economics, hold the key to foreign policy and its reception elsewhere. What we are dealing with is the undulation of power and discontent, of superordinate and subordinate relationships. And it is hard to deny the conclusion that as long as nations behave as surrogate persons, assuming the characteristics of power and powerlessness, no complete resolution of the policy questions can occur.

Once again, we must understand that the problem is one of perception: can any small or medium-sized nation feel secure and in a condition of equity when confronted by a superpower such as the United States? Can any set of actions or pronouncements be greeted with anything less than universal suspicion? I rather suspect that the emotive drive behind the charges of imperialism stem, in considerable part, not from the conduct of specific policies, but from the implicit clout behind the nation asserting such policies. In this, we have ample precedent, not just in the history of European colonies, but in the present period as well. There is Cuba's hostility to China; Algeria's response to France; Rhodesia's response to England; Yugoslavia's response to the Soviet Union. It is not that real oppression does not exist. The outbursts of small powers against big powers are often based on hard fact. Further, superpowers are not the same and small powers' claims are of varying magnitudes. Claims to our sympathies and support cannot be eliminated by an awareness of big-power chauvinism. The point is entirely beyond that: as long as superpower exists, resentments based on disequilibrium of power and wealth will remain a constant fact of political life.

III. National Interests and Multinational Corporations

The rise of the multinational corporation illustrates how limited the federal foreign policy role has become. Although still largely dominated by United States industrial units, international combines in the fields of petroleum, chemistry, and electrical energy stimulate direct contacts between the corporate structures and the political leadership of Latin American nations. Venezuela makes agreements with Standard Oil, Chile deals directly with Anaconda Copper, Peru arranges meetings with the Council for Latin America, Inc. (a collectivity of more than two hundred United States firms representing more than 30 percent of our investments in the area). The Nixon Doctrine of maintaining a "low profile" in the hemisphere is directly connected to the reemergence of the entrepreneurial hard sell. Whatever this might signify in the larger context—a return to neo-isolationism or simply a faith in the supremacy of capitalism with or without democracy—it is evident that at this juncture official United States foreign policy counts for considerably less than at any time in the twentieth century, or certainly since the presidency of Herbert Hoover.

United States foreign policy clout is limited by the rise of nationalism politically and the emergence of multi-national corporativism economically. The increased pressure within Latin America for national control of the industrial base reflects a double tendency: the maturation of a domestic bourgeoisie rather than a foreign controlled economic consortium. This limitation on United States policy-making has been accelerated by the depoliticalization of industrial linkages generally; that is to say, the rise of the multi-national corporation has subjected economic relations to technical personnel and fiscal considerations removed from the old-fashioned use of economic domination for political ends.

If imperialism could have been ended by diplomatic maneuver or popular acclaim, United States interests in Latin America would long since have been eliminated. But the process of nationalizing industry raises as many problems as it resolves. Compensating the former owner may simply not be worth the costs, and as in Chile, mixed companies might be superior. But seizure without compensation might so alienate the former colonial power that it denies the Latin American nation access to United States and European banking credit, cuts off the supply of capital goods and technology, and pressures the other advanced countries to deny the expropriating nation any international development loans. What adds salt to the wound is that, again as in the case of Chile, the denial of the copper yield to the United States may prove meaningless—since Chilean copper mainly supplies the needs of Western Europe and Japan. Again, just what United States foreign policy can do in such a situation is problematic; at the most, it can support the claims of its own capitalist entrepreneurs, and at the least, it can work out the equitable grounds for the transition from foreign to domestic ownership of mineral wealth and factory produce. Of course, in the absence of a policy the United States can do nothing—its usual type of "action."

There is a widespread belief that United States foreign policy toward Latin America is both more rigorous and more extensive than it is toward other parts of the Third World. The argument claims that there is a special tutelary relationship between the United States and Latin America, and hence a much tougher stance toward our hemispheric neighbors than toward other areas. I would submit that this is not entirely true. What does, in fact, exist is a tough corporate policy of American giants of industry toward Latin America. That is to say, after years of struggle against foreign corporate interests, the United States has emerged as the strongest of foreign investors in the private sector. General Motors has prevailed over Fiat and Peugeot in the automobile sector, Pratt & Whitney has ousted Rolls Royce in the aircraft engine market, Ford-Philco dominates the television field over Phillips of the Netherlands, Colgate-Palmolive Peet is supreme in the bathroom utensils field, etc. However, this may change with the penetration of Japanese and German products expressly geared to Latin Americans' purchasing power.

These United States corporate interests were powerful long before the United States forged a unified policy toward the Latin Americans. Thus, the federal foreign policy sector has long been the tail being wagged by the corporate dog. If there is precious little in United States foreign policy in general, its scantiness in Latin America is downright notorious; at every turn, United States policy has been dictated to and overruled by United States corporate interests: oil interests dictated United States foreign policy in Mexico to the point of collapsing the Good Neighbor Policy of the New Deal period. International Telephone and Telegraph anger over attempts to expropriate its interests in Brazil in itself caused a worsening of the United States attitude toward the Goulart regime in the early 1960s. Similarly, the Anaconda and Kennecott copper interests have done more to dissuade the United States government from establishing friendly relations with the new Chilean regime than any other single influence. What we have, then, is the making of foreign policy, but more by the private corporate sector than by the federal public sector.

What makes the relationship between the United States and Latin America special, and what makes foreign policy so difficult in this area of the world, is that with Latin America, the United States is dealing with people, many of whom identify more strongly with the Western world rather than with a Third World. The interests of Latin America, Asia, and Africa coincide far less frequently than revolutionary rhetoric claims. To say that they all suffer from imperialism and colonialism is simply insufficient, especially if imperialism is itself a differential response revealing changing tactical requirements. Latin America has a long tradition of constitutionalism, bourgeois economic control, ultra-nationalistic quests, and countervailing demands for world power. All of this makes Latin America far from the subordinate hemisphere that it once was—whether we are dealing with bourgeois or socialist regimes, democratic or undemocratic regimes, Latin America displays a much more powerful clustering of nations, a more forceful presentation of national self-interests, than do other parts of the Third World. In all of this, one would have to say that the continuing warfare of the United States on Southeast Asia has had the uniform effect of hardening attitudes, and of making it clear somehow that the age of gunboat diplomacy is over. In this sense, there seems to be a growing feeling that the United States intervention in the Dominican Republic in 1965 ended a chapter of American military history that began with the invasion of Nicaragua in 1912. And the Vietnam War has profoundly underscored this fact. The United States which could only manage to achieve a draw in Korea in the fifties and to lose in Vietnam in the sixties can no longer expect acquiescence even from the most subservient Latin American regime. Indeed, the very bottleneck that Vietnam represents for the United States has merely served to underscore the absence of an overall United States policy; overextension in the Asian conflict has necessarily shrunk its commitment to Latin America.

IV. Latin American Nationalism and North American Paternalism

The end of World War II, and the Chapultepec Conference that followed, not only failed to signal the end of Latin American distrust of the United States, but brought to the surface differences buried by the war, and ended the profits Latin American businessmen made from it. Differences of opinion emerged on every major policy front after World War II and remained unresolved: tariff protection, foreign capital domination in Latin American enterprises, government intervention in economic affairs, the need for multilateral finance mechanisms in place of existing bilateral mechanisms. In addition, there was a strong difference of emphasis on the crucial subject of planning and the public sector.

The aim of every American president from Truman to Nixon

has been the same: not only to abolish Latin American economic dependency on non-American producers, but in the same process to establish Latin American dependence upon the United States. Insofar as this is a policy, then the United States has a policy.

But in establishing such a model of dependency certain tactical problems arose. Should the United States base its foreign policy on an economic model of free enterprise and private property, or should it place its bets on a military model of government assistance? The private enterprise versus the military appropriations approach has become the crucial divide among policy-makers interested in formulating a Latin American policy. Obviously, such problems will ever remain unresolved, to the extent that Latin America has moved beyond a dependency model to begin with.

State Department officials like Spruille Braden and John Foster Dulles ranked the institution of private property alongside religion and the family as a bulwark of civilization. Needless to add, their beliefs were translated into the cornerstones of American foreign policy. In contrast, George C. Marshall, Bernard Baruch, Will Clayton, and Averell Harriman began to note that the real problem was military control and not economic control. As the military situation tightened up throughout the Third World, the Pentagon began to win out over the Brookings Institution in forming a strategy for Latin America. Later agreements, such as the Rio Pact, began to stress the role of the military—not as an international check against communism, but as an internal check against unsponsored social change. The Bogota Conference of 1948 went even further toward securing political concessions from Latin America in exchange for slender economic concessions from the United States.

With the assertion of independence by elites after World War II, which took the form of a re-emergence of nationalism in Bolivia in 1952, Guatemala in 1954, Cuba in 1959, the Dominican Republic in 1965, Peru and Bolivia again in 1968, and Chile in 1970, the idea of imperial military solutions or military solidarity between Latin and United States officers broke down. The Latin American military increasingly became attached to middle class nationalist aspirations and decreasingly attached to overseas American commitments. As a result, Nixon's Action for Progress looks much like the earlier Roosevelt Good Neighbor Policy with its emphasis on private investment and private initiative. United States foreign policy, whatever its overall consistency at the level of principles, is badly polarized at the tactical level between economic laissez faire doctrine and military interventionist policies. The resolution of this policy dilemma no longer lies within the power of the United States government, but rather is a function of the internal dynamics of Latin American social classes and political movements on one side, and of the changing character of industrial ownership and management on the other.

This regional approach has always added a special dimension to United States relationships with Latin America. Every rebellion has appeared as treason, and every revolutionary nationalist seemed to come across as a Robert E. Lee seeking to take his state out of the Union. In other words, the very proximity in geography and history has led to a special sort of policy-response—a response based on the assumption that what Latin America did was part of domestic policy. It has taken Castro in Cuba, Allende in Chile, and the military *golpistas* of Peru and Bolivia to make it clear that things have changed in the Western hemisphere and in the world, and that the nations of Latin America do not wish to become part of a statehood or commonwealth program. Even little Puerto Rico, long a United States satrapy, has become restless. Indeed, the very shock of recognition that Latin America, left, right, or center, is not part of the United States may finally lead to an appropriate foreign policy posture.

V. Concluding Utopianisms: A Return to Innocence

There is a strong movement afoot to think of democracy in far less representational and far more participatory terms. This extends beyond the borders of the United States and is manifested in the rise of community-control orientations and open-ended ethical frameworks in which, as Nehru once said, each man, and not just each nation, is entitled to make mistakes. This movement envisages a world in which patriotism, jingoism, flag-waving, and all outward signs of imposed deference to national authority are beginning to lose their omnipotence. That such a movement is far more extensive in the powerful nation-states is certainly understandable; for it is in such nations that nationalism is oldest and has been most binding and most repressive. But the movement against nationalism has spread throughout the world.

Jordan and Israel may growl at each other, but Israeli and Jordanian youth are interacting with each other nonetheless. The United States and the People's Republic of China may be years away from negotiating a diplomatic *détente,* but the devotees of table tennis are yet able to connect up in meaningful competition. Diplomats, who during the day posture and growl at each other, in the evening tell one another the miserable truths about themselves and their nations, and drink concoctions of vodka mixed with Coke in careful derision of their implausible countries with their rigid restrictions. I am not suggesting that these isolated outbursts of humanity will triumph over foreign policy formations, although, God knows, that would not be such a bad outcome. I am suggesting that there is something irrepressible about the human will. And this irrepressibility is probably more important than a ton of diplomatic papers and an equal weight of United Nations resolutions.

The likelihood is that the same revolution that is sweeping American society will sweep world society: a revolution, not of rising expectations, not necessarily even one of falling profits— nothing so ostentatious and pretentious as that—but rather a revolution of the person, a revolution that is based on the knowledge that every individual counts as one, that every individual has the right to pursue life unimpeded and unthreatened by either secular power or clerical ideology. Every man will make his own foreign policy: every man will make his own peace with the children of Vietnam; every woman will make her own peace with the children of South Africa; and every child will make his own peace with every other child of the world. If this sounds a frantically utopian conclusion to a prosaic topic, so be it. Eventually, foreign policy must be an activity each person somehow is able to engage in. Up to the present, we have been content with a foreign policy that was vaguely responsive. Now this is simply not enough. Foreign policy must be something brought down to size. Every person must decide with whom to interact and with whom not to interact. Every person must be able to decide, however complex and difficult the chore, how much should be allocated to whom, by whom, and why. When every man is a sovereign power, the very distinction between domestic and foreign policy will vanish. The choice between the Anarch and the Behemoth is central—the denial of the right to the democratic control of foreign policy is already a surrender to state power, and such a surrender will mean not only an inability of ordinary people to control policy, but a loss of whatever we mean by mass politics as such.

I am going to avoid any bombastic call for the revision of United States foreign policy, since as I suggested at the outset, I seriously doubt the existence of such an entity. Even if a foreign policy does exist, it is too vacuous really to alter. Nor shall I fall into the opposite temptation of declaring everything in such a stable state as to require no changes of behavior or approaches. The closer to the subject I get, the more convinced I am that the answers to problems such as the foreign policy of the United States are not to be found in a statement of particular ways in which policies can be improved. At some level, no matter what changes of policy are pronounced or promulgated, it will be less than satisfactory since it will leave intact the fundamental division between superordinate and subordinate states. Thus the problem is not the existence of a United States foreign policy but more radically the existence of a United States or the existence of a Latin America. Those opposed to the United States will not be made happy by an enunciation of positive steps, while those fervently dedicated to United States first principles will believe that only through emulation of United States practices and premises will Latin American ills be cured.

The statist solution is therefore no solution. People will have to connect up with each other in dramatic new ways: people will link up on professional grounds, seeing each other functionally in terms of common problems of engineering, architecture, student life, etc. People will have to see each other in terms of shared problems generated by different systems; living under capitalism or under socialism will become a source for new discourse and analysis. In short, when foreign policy and domestic policy no longer present a sharp bifurcation, it is possible that the topic discussed will be resolved. Like most problems, that of American foreign policy will not be resolved so much as be outflanked by a series of new issues that grip the imagination and attention of men and movements.

There is one lesson to be learned from business elements working in Latin America: the possibility of working through problems without regard to government policy makers. In a sense, this same tactic has to be extended to all other groups. There must be a concerted effort to link up for common tasks: social scientists with social scientists, surgeons with surgeons, engineers with engineers, and radical politicians with radical politicans. For it is precisely such linkages at a human level that, while extremely difficult to establish, are at least still possible. These human linkages must not be a simple function of bureaucratic mechanisms such as the Peace Corps or any other extension of the federal arm. It is hard to believe that one hundred years of superordinate-subordinate relations in the hemisphere are really going to be altered through the benign action of governments. It is much easier to believe that improved communication between scholars, politicians, technicians, and professional personnel will make possible new forms of association that will prove to be a meaningful bridge over troubled waters.

United States Policy in Southeast Asia

Allen S. Whiting

NOTHING SEEMS MORE impossible a problem for the average citizen today than United States policy in Southeast Asia. Without obvious boundary lines in space, time, or frame of reference, he must consider Vietnam, China, and the world-wide credibility of the United States commitment. He must understand how past presidents got us where we are, the present president's prospects of success and failure, and what we hope to see after the Vietnam War ends. Finally, he can evaluate and prescribe policy on the basis of international law, or national interests, or personal morality, but not all three, because they do not agree.

And even if we can cope with these multi-faceted questions, we somehow sense a futile irrelevance to our effort. If the millions of man-hours and tons of print expended on United States policy in Southeast Asia over the past decade, spanning the Taylor-Rostow mission of President Kennedy of 1961 and the Laos incursion of President Nixon in 1971, still leave this nation wracked and riven, what can further public discussion hope to accomplish? Should we not simply trust that men in Washington, Saigon, Phnom Penh, Vientiane, and Hanoi will "muddle through" somehow and solve the problem for us?

These seem reasonable questions to ask in this, the seventh year since United States aircraft first bombed the Democratic Republic of Vietnam in a futile effort to stop that country's attack against the Republic of Vietnam. But reasonable questions may not encourage reasonable answers and any response which favors abandoning the future to fate or leaving it to the men who have already brought affairs to their present sorry state must be rejected. So long as we are a democracy with duly-elected representatives in the Congress and in the White House, we must persist in holding those men responsible for the consequences of their action or inaction in the wielding of United States power abroad. No matter how we may weary of the effort or despair of the results, it is our obligation to assess our policy and to explore alternatives which may hold lesser costs even if they do not promise greater gains.

I. The Issues Posed

In short, we must ask, what have we done in Southeast Asia? What did we set out to do? And should we keep on as we are? The sequence is important if we are to assess policy responsibility, not in terms of its own objectives alone although we shall consider these as well, but first of all in terms of its consequences. The road to hell *is* paved with good intentions, especially in domestic and foreign politics. Looking at our positive accomplishments since our active entry into Southeast Asian affairs with the first Geneva Conference of 1954, we can credibly claim to have kept most of South Vietnam and one-third of Laos out of Communist control. This much is indisputable. But we cannot claim more than this, either for the countries of Indo-China or elsewhere on the mainland and throughout the island archipelago. We have not built any stable lasting peace or any viable political systems in Indo-China. We have not made the region internally cohesive. We cannot even credibly claim to have decisively affected the prospects for insurgency, Communist or otherwise, in Burma, Thailand, Malaysia, and Indonesia. Only in the Philippines can United States policy point, albeit perhaps more with shame than pride, to the low ebb of local revolt despite the shocking state of the political and economic systems which cry out for change.

Moreover, we must go beyond this accounting of positive accomplishments and lack thereof. We must also credit United States policy in Southeast Asia since 1961 with having killed, maimed, and made civilians homeless on a scale unknown in the modern history of Southeast Asia. United States policy has overtly as well as covertly violated international treaties, laws, and customs without the slightest pretense of prior agreement with local governments or reference to the obligations undertaken as a founding member of the United Nations.

We have done all this while destroying one president, threatening the future of a second, and crushing the confidence of many of our young people in the values and goals which Americans have traditionally avowed both at home and throughout the world—such values as honesty, responsibility, and above all, humanity. What is the difference between My Lai and Lidice? between Thanh Haa and Madrid? between napalm and mustard gas? True, we cannot fully compare our war crimes with those of other nations. They did not have cameramen and reporters covering war without censorship. But we can compare the testimony of a Lieutenant Calley with our sense of ourselves and ask: What *has* United States policy wrought in Southeast Asia?

If this is what we set out to do, then surely we must be saving the peoples of Indo-China from a fate worse than death since we so freely bring death to those peoples every day. Is that fate communism? Apparently not, since we are content to let the National Liberation Front compete in elections, possibly winning control of the Saigon government. At least this is what we proclaim at Paris. Is that fate control from Hanoi? Again we must answer in the negative, since we do not oppose the peaceful unification of Vietnam, or so we also proclaim at Paris. Are we merely fighting for the principle of peaceful self-determination, free from outside interference? We proclaim this as well, but we cannot convince others that this objective vindicates our use of force to defeat the only rice-roots movements with genuine popular support, whether forced or voluntary, in Laos and South Vietnam. Moreover, fighting fire with fire seems an insane strategy when the resulting conflagration burns down the town and many of its inhabitants.

In short, none of these rationales suffices although all of them have been used at one time or another. Instead, the only consistent and comprehensible explanation for United States policy in Southeast Asia is "the containment of Communist China." Secretary of State Dean Rusk was not alone in this view, although he stated it more bluntly than others. From President Eisenhower and Secretary Dulles through President Johnson, the shadow of China loomed large over Southeast Asia in United States policy statements.[1] Whether it is the dramatic image of "dominos"

1. William P. Bundy, "New Tides in Southeast Asia," *Foreign Affairs* (January 1971), confirms that "in the spring and summer of 1965, when the culminating series of major American decisions in Viet-

falling to Chinese control or the subtle suggestion of Peking's "influence" bringing Southeast Asia under Chinese domination, the ultimate justification for an American policy of military treaties, bases, subversion, and war is "the Chinese threat."

Superficially, at least, this "containment" policy might seem logical enough. Although Hanoi has fought the Indo-China war, off and on, for twenty-five years—first against the French and then the United States—it is Peking that has furnished most of the weapons, ammunition, and political support.[2] North Vietnam has neither the capacity nor the will to conquer all Southeast Asia, but China clearly can pump sufficient men and munitions into Communist insurgencies, should it so choose, to make eventual conquest certain in the absence of any outside intervention. Nor were Chinese verbal and material demonstrations of "support for national liberation struggles" reassuring in this regard, at least in the early 1950s. That United States policy concerns were Chinese and not merely communism *per se* was shown in Indonesia. There Washington acquiesced in the ever-growing role of the Indonesian Communist party, allied with President Sukarno who proclaimed a "Pyongyang-Peking-Jakarta axis." But Indonesia lay far beyond China's landlocked legions, unlike the mainland of Southeast Asia. Its politics might be deplored but they were not to be confronted with United States arms, as in Laos, Thailand, and South Vietnam.

Stripped of its verbiage, then, United States policy in Southeast Asia has sought to save it from domination by Peking. This raises several basic questions. First, is the area genuinely threatened by China? If so, does this affect United States interests? And if both questions are answered affirmatively, are there feasible means for thwarting that threat that are consonant with present United States policy or with reasonable alternatives?

---

nam was taken . . . a Hanoi takeover of South Vietnam seemed likely, in conjunction with other trends, to make probable . . . a wave of Chinese expansion into the rest of Southeast Asia."

2. Official sources estimated that arms caches seized in Cambodia revealed 60 percent of the weapons and 80 percent of the ammunition to have been of Chinese manufacture. Beginning in late 1965, Chinese weapons replaced the potpourri of captured and homemade equipment previously used by Communist forces in South Vietnam in all categories up to and including mortars, with only the larger rocket launchers coming from the Soviet Union.

II.   The "Chinese Threat": Southeast Asian Views

We can, and have, used various criteria for determining the nature and extent of a Chinese threat to Southeast Asia, including statements by Southeast Asian leaders, pronouncements from Peking, and so-called "hard facts" of Chinese behavior in the area. So far as Southeast Asian spokesmen are concerned, it is easier to find anti-Chinese views than a will to unite against Peking. This suggests either that different things are meant by "the Chinese threat" or that different policies are preferred to meet it, or both. For example, American officials and journalists in the Philippines or Indonesia readily elicit a vigorous affirmative response to the question, "Do you believe China poses a threat?", but this is more likely to reflect hostility to local or "overseas" Chinese than fear of Peking. Such prejudice frequently leads to persecution, if not outright suppression, of Chinese communities in these countries. However, when it comes to United States policy in Indo-China, Indonesia has been consistent in its opposition, if varied in its expression thereof as between the public diatribes of Sukarno and the more private demurrers of his successors. As for the Philippines, such active support as we have gained there for Vietnam has been more the result of United States dollars than a desire to contain Chinese Communist expansionism.

To be sure, racial prejudice and fear of economic domination by Chinese money-lenders and traders can combine with a genuine threat of subversion from Peking. Thus, traditional Malay hostility to and fear of Chinese ascendancy received fresh impetus with the still simmering insurgency, almost wholly Chinese in composition and clearly dependent upon Peking and its Southeast Asian network for guidance and material support. Malay's ability to unite, if only for a few years, with the predominantly Chinese city of Singapore showed an ability to differentiate local Chinese, Communist, and mainland Chinese issues. Since the ouster of Singapore from Malaysia, however, the issues are once again blurred.

Thailand, by contrast, shows sufficient assimilation and cooption between the Thai bureaucratic elite and the Chinese commercial community to remove virtually all threat of subversion through this minority group. Thai strictures against the

Chinese threat are more complicated. On the one hand, they reflect genuine apprehension that Peking's support for dissident Thai politicians in exile, for neglected or oppressed minority peoples in the disadvantaged northern provinces, and for an avowed Thai Communist party, can combine to forge a united insurgent movement of serious proportions. Should this movement link with parallel efforts mounted from Hanoi amongst disaffected groups in northeast Thailand, enjoying easy access across the Mekong to Pathet Lao as well as North Vietnamese bases, the total threat could become as serious as that which confronted South Vietnam.[3]

On the other hand, Thai ambivalence over the best foreign policy response suggests a more complicated situation than is apparent in the echo-chamber enlargement of American views dutifully reported from Bangkok. As between Peking and Hanoi, the greater perceived threat, judging by Thai behavior, is from North Vietnam via Laos. Indeed, intimations of a possible *détente* between Bangkok and Peking emerged in the mid-fifties, actively pursued by Chou En-lai at the Bandung Conference. Should United States policy reduce or remove American force from the mainland of Southeast Asia, one strong Thai sentiment will be for a reassurance agreement with China to mitigate further pressures from Indo-China.

This is, of course, the policy pursued by Prince Sihanouk for more than a decade, whereby he actively sought Chinese aid to check Vietnamese encroachment.[4] Although any serious hope of Peking moving against Hanoi was an obvious illusion, he nonetheless beefed up Cambodia's miniscule military force with Chinese weapons while seeking Peking's approval for his border claims against South Vietnam, claims that clearly affected the aspirations of Hanoi. Still another view has been that of Burma, where the Chinese threat is explicit in the form of public and private backing for the dissident Burmese Communist party, as well

3. David S. Wilson, *The United States and the Future of Thailand* (New York: Frederick A. Praeger, Inc., 1970) presents the most comprehensive analysis of the various insurgencies and minority divisions.
4. Roger M. Smith, *Cambodia's Foreign Policy* (Ithaca, N.Y.: Cornell University Press, 1966) provides a sensitive understanding of Prince Sihanouk's politics.

as for separatist Kachins battling government troops along the Chinese border. This border provides twelve hundred miles of opportunity for covert support to any of the several insurgencies resisting Rangoon's authority. It is small wonder then, that under these circumstances, Burmese officials seldom speak to outsiders about "the Chinese threat" and then only in discreet whispers. Instead they have chosen direct diplomacy, negotiating a tacit *modus vivendi* with Peking paralleling that of Finland and the Soviet Union, although unlike Finland no legitimate political figure or party in Burma espouses the ideology of its neighbor.

This necessarily superficial survey serves to illustrate the variable content of "the Chinese threat" as articulated in Southeast Asia. If "proof" of the "threat" depends on statements of Southeast Asian leaders, the argument is specious. Worse, it can be circular to the extent that these leaders either accept our assertions as based on better intelligence and analysis than they have concerning Chinese Communist ability and intent, or parrot our analysis back for its manipulative use in winning American support for their personal or national interests. Educated for twenty years to the economic as well as the political benefits of agreeing with Washington on the perfidy of Peking, some elites are unlikely to differ openly with us on this question, regardless of their private calculations to the contrary. Others may believe our diagnoses of the problem but reject our prescription for solution.

III. United States Views

Just as Southeast Asian views vary, so too does the Chinese threat as defined by United States policy. At one extreme, with the fewest adherents and the least credibility, is the spectre of invasion by a population of 750 million. Although Secretary Rusk enlarged on this extreme by coupling the implicit image of Chinese "hordes" with explicit reference to Peking's possession of nuclear weapons, his view has not been shared by most policy planners. At the opposite extreme is the notion reflected in President Nixon's recent State of the World message which singles out Chinese "hegemony" as something we must resist.[5] This concept is so vague and susceptible to several definitions as not to

5. President Richard M. Nixon, *United States Foreign Policy for the 1970's* (Washington, D. C., 1971).

inspire any particular policy. Least of all is it able to justify the sacrifice of lives and wealth in order to forestall political influence which inevitably accompanies propinquity and power in international relations. The hollowness of this rationale was evident in President Nixon's claim that four "powers" will compete for influence in the area, hopefully counterbalancing the possible ascendency of any one of them.[6] His citing of Japan can be challenged since Japan lacks any present or prospective military force in Southeast Asia, as can the Soviet Union whose primary interests will remain limited to the Middle East and possibly the Indian subcontinent. This leaves only the United States and China, with the vagaries of the Nixon Doctrine no substitute for Peking's inherent advantages so far as influence—as opposed to control—is concerned.

Secretaries Dulles and Rusk had Peking in mind, however, when they tried to stop Hanoi's use of force as "indirect Chinese aggression" and "war by proxy." Earlier visions of a Sino-Soviet "bloc" and a "monolith" run by Moscow had enabled Secretary of State Dean Acheson to deny the Chinese Communists were an indigenous, independent force in 1949.[7] So, too, did Dulles and Rusk imply that Ho Chi Minh was merely a front man for Mao Tse-tung. It mattered little that official files in Washington had ample evidence of Mao's disputes with Stalin, and suggested North Vietnamese resentment over Chinese policies.[8] Basically

6. Bundy, op. cit., offers a more sophisticated variant of this theme.
7. *United States Relations With China* (Department of State, Washington, D. C., 1949); see "Letter of Transmittal" by Secretary of State Dean Acheson, "The Communist leaders have foresworn their Chinese heritage and have publicly announced their subservience to a foreign power. . . . Foreign domination has been masked behind the facade of a vast crusading movement which apparently has seemed to many Chinese to be wholly indigenous and national." Acheson omits these portions from his excerpts quoted in his memoir, *Present At The Creation* (New York: W. W. Norton and Co., 1969).
8. For evidence of differences between the Chinese and Russian Communists, see *Foreign Relations of the United States, 1945, vol. VII, The Far East: China* (Department of State, Washington, D. C. 1969), especially pp. 279-83 and 368-71. While less documentation is available on the later Hanoi-Peking tension, some illumination is thrown on this question by a former "insider," Chester Cooper, *The Lost Crusade* (New York: Dodd, Mead & Co., 1970), and by

these were all Communists, and since Communism was known to require a single center, control obviously went to the possessor of greater power, from Hanoi to Peking, and from Peking to Moscow. Even when the Sino-Soviet dispute shattered this illusion, its proponents persisted in applying it to relations between North Vietnam and China.

This myth dies hard, but die it must if there is to be any end to the Indo-China War that involves a compromise settlement with Hanoi. Ironically, China's influence may have been decisive in bringing North Vietnamese leaders to accept the 1954 Geneva agreements instead of pursuing their military advantages further in Vietnam.[9] However, it is one thing to withhold essential support as leverage for inducing a cease-fire, and quite another to offer support as an incentive to fight. Ho Chi Minh's willingness to pursue the Indo-China war in the face of steadily escalating United States military opposition cannot, by any stretch of the imagination, have represented forced submission to Mao Tse-tung. On the contrary, Hanoi has repeatedly bargained with Moscow and negotiated at Paris in clear defiance of Peking's advice. If we seriously intend to negotiate with North Vietnam, we must recognize it has interests which it considers as legitimate and separable from those of China. Both may agree on the removal of United States bases from Southeast Asia, but North Vietnam's interests also include the union of the Indo-Chinese peoples under the leadership of Hanoi, not Peking.

A stronger case for a Chinese threat lies in the subversion and insurgency of Communist parties whose inspiration and material support come largely from China. Among these the most prominent are the Burmese, Thai, and Malayan movements. The Indonesian Communist party is so decimated as not to be recognizable in its few surviving self-appointed spokesmen in Peking. There is no question that *Peking Review* touts these armed insurrections as foreshadowing victorious "national liberation" struggles, that Radio Peking broadcasts inflammatory messages to incite local

a scholar, Melvin Gurtov, *The First Vietnam Crisis* (New York: Columbia University Press, 1967).

9. Gurtov, ibid. Chou En-lai told James Reston, "We were very badly taken in during the first Geneva conference." *New York Times*, 10 August 1971. This self-criticism may well reflect Hanoi's judgment as well.

support of communist rebels, and that money, munitions, and manpower train and equip such insurgents in Chinese base camps. Moreover, such support is forthcoming whether the local government, like Burma, enjoys good diplomatic relations with China, or hostile relations, as with Thailand. Finally, it makes no difference whether the rebels have a long history of failure, as in Burma, or came into action only during the Vietnam War, again as in Thailand. Apparently Peking's door is always open to those who claim to follow Mao's path of armed struggle in the countryside and to mouth his maxim, "Power comes from the barrel of a gun." Since 1960 an additional Chinese requirement has been to take Peking's side against Moscow in the Sino-Soviet dispute, but this probably has not bothered most Southeast Asian Communists who have had little reason to expect Russian help against local governments.

IV. The Chinese View

The critical variable here does not seem to be China's willingness to back local insurgency but rather the ability of these insurgents to organize their forces and to mobilize the populace against the regime.[10] If they lack organization, as in Burma, or mobilizing appeal, as in Thailand, they remain a potential but not a serious danger. For its part, Peking's willingness to support such movements has never gone much beyond what local recruitment could justify. Except in Vietnam, no significant manpower contributions, despite the presence of identical linguistic and ethnic groups in China, have crossed the border to assist insurrections in Southeast Asia. At a higher theoretical level, Lin Piao's famous pamphlet *On People's Wars,* is virtually a "do it yourself" manual which abjures local Communists against expecting outside material aid, as differentiated from political and moral support.[11]

It is important to note that the modest levels of Chinese support for revolutionary struggles abroad cannot be credited to

10. Peter Van Ness, *Revolution and Chinese Foreign Policy* (Berkeley: University of California Press, 1970), examines Chinese theory and practice in support of "wars of national liberation."
11. David P. Mozingo and Thomas W. Robinson, *Lin Piao on "People's War,"* The RAND Corporation, Research Memorandum RM-4814-PR, November 1965.

constraints imposed by United States policy.[12] Since the creation
of SEATO in 1954, unaligned Burma has suffered no greater subversive pressures from China than has aligned Thailand. The
Malayan movement remains a troublesome nuisance in Sarawak
as in the peninsula, but Peking seems no more willing to raise its
level of support here than where United States commitments are
absent as compared with the Philippines where we are committed.
Indonesia moved from near takeover by the Communists who
headed the largest political movement, to massive massacres of all
associated with the movement, without major intervention from
Peking at any stage. Indeed, the tenuous nature of Peking's
affiliation with and responsibility for particular levels of
insurgency in given countries at any point in time makes especially hazardous efforts to establish causal linkages between this
interaction and United States policy, either actual or as perceived in Peking.

In sum, Chinese policy seems to be one of genuine self-restraint.
The mixture of motives certainly includes theoretical considerations of revolutionary success being basically predicated on local
conditions rather than external assistance. Practical calculation
may also seek to avoid a possible nationalistic backlash against
too much foreign participation, especially where Chinese as well
as China are viewed with suspicion as they tend to be in Southeast Asia. In addition, a traditional long time perspective can
argue against attempting impatiently to force historical developments, rather than letting them take their own course. Happily,
from Peking's viewpoint, this point is "proven" by the three
decades of struggle from the Chinese Communist party's birth in
1921 to its triumph in 1949. Finally, Chinese ethnocentrism tends
to place domestic objectives first. Prior needs for national defense
against external threats as well as for mobilizing internal
resources in pursuit of economic development constrain the will
and the capacity to pursue revolutionary objectives abroad.

Whatever the mixture and relative weight of motives, the consequence is to downgrade sharply the nature and extent of

12. An excellent overview of the area by a detached British scholar is
    provided by Peter Lyon, *War and Peace in Southeast Asia* (New
    York: Oxford University Press, 1969).

China's threat manifested through insurgent movements in Southeast Asia.[13] More than this the notion that peace in the area, whether domestic or international, would be possible if there were *no* interference from China simply does not accord with reality, past, present, or prospective. Only Thailand can trace its unbroken existence as a national entity through recent history, with all that implies for social cohesion and a consciousness of unity. However, even here Lao and Vietnamese minorities, Meo hill peoples, and traditional bandits limit central government authority and, in times of economic trouble, react violently against officials. Elsewhere, colonialism left its stamp with artificial boundaries and alienated populaces, supposedly subject to the sovereign rule of whatever intellectualized elite was left behind to rule the state.[14] Whether the problem is one of ethnic differences as among the Shans, Karens, and Kachins of Burma, or of regional conflicts as between Sumatra and Java in Indonesia, the seeds of political resistance and armed revolt were sown by British, French, and Dutch rule—not by Mao's Chinese Communist colleagues.

Nor are the region's international conflicts any more the creation of Peking. Enmity between Burman and Thai, Thai and Cambodian, Cambodian and Vietnamese, Filipino and Malay, Malay and Indonesian long antedate arrival of the colonial powers. They were further exacerbated by the heritage of colonialism with its artificial divisions reflecting competitive metropole rule and its legalistic insistence that all resulting boundaries were sacrosanct, regardless of their historical, cultural, or ethnic basis. Add to this the inevitable testing of the international pecking order which associates prestige with pretensions to power and one can understand how various tensions

13. A tightly argued analysis of Chinese considerations in the area may be found in Melvin Gurtov, *Southeast Asia Tomorrow* (Baltimore: The Johns Hopkins Press, 1970), drawing from a major unpublished work by Gurtov examining in detail Chinese policies toward Burma, Thailand, and Cambodia during the decade 1958-68.

14. John P. Cady, *Southeast Asia: Its Historical Development* (New York: McGraw-Hill, 1964), gives an encyclopaedic account; for brief article surveys by competent scholars, see the anthology, *Man, State, and Society in Contemporary Southeast Asia*, edited by Robert O. Tilman, (New York: Frederick A. Praeger, Inc., 1969).

affect the states of Southeast Asia in their relations with one another, China wholly apart.[15]

But China is *not* wholly apart. Its traditional relations with the area were intimate if permissive. Having lost "suzerain" domination to European colonial rule in the nineteenth century, twentieth-century China leaders were determined to re-establish an overlordship that seemed their proper right in terms both of historical precedent and the self-perceived innate superiority of China. Such pretensions conflict with the theoretical equality of states under international law, but they parallel large state behavior toward proximate smaller states as is amply evident on the part of the United States and the Soviet Union.

Much has been made of Chinese Communist references to "lost territories" and to maps published in Peking which delimit the furthest reaches of past empire as embracing most of Southeast Asia. Less is said of identical statements by Chiang Kai-shek and similar maps published under his mainland rule.[16] It would be absurd in either case to identify this as evidence of latent "Chinese expansionism" which is merely awaiting the opportunity to rule other countries either by annexation or as full-fledged satellites. It would be equally absurd, however, to disregard this evidence of self-defined roles and responsibilities, consequent from being the largest nation in Asia. China's traditional title of *Chung Kuo,* or Middle Kingdom, correctly betokens this aspiration to ascendancy over its lesser neighbors.

Given this outlook, it would be no surprise were Peking to exploit the extant international conflicts in the area to its own advantage, as did Germany in Eastern Europe and Russia in the Middle East. Actually, Chinese interference in and exacerbation of international disputes in Southeast Asia is more notable for its absence than for its presence. The communist ideological component, with its emphasis on the need as well as the desirability to exploit contradictions, both internal and external, to defend China and the "liberation struggle" against "reactionary oppression and imperialism," adds further impetus to fish in troubled waters. Fortunately, Chinese self-restraint in the face of the

---

15. Bernard K. Gordon, *The Dimensions of Conflict in Southeast Asia* (Englewood Cliffs, N.J.: Prentice-Hall, Inc., 1966).
16. Chiang Kai-shek, *China's Destiny* (New York: Roy Publishers, Inc., 1947), especially pp. 34-5.

inevitable and inherent difficulties facing the countries of Southeast Asia render absurd the "worst case" nightmares conjured up by various hypothetical projections of the "Chinese threat."

Lest this be misunderstood, we must add that Peking deserves no praise for causing less trouble than it might. Neither is there any basis for arguing that if China were Nationalist instead of Communist the same degree and kind of interference in Southeast Asian affairs would occur. Finally, there is no need for approving every level of meddling as justifiable within a larger power's "sphere of interest." But these caveats aside, it is important to shade into proper perspective the absolute alternatives posed by such terms as "peace in Southeast Asia" versus "domination by China."

Thus in answer to our first question, "is the area genuinely threatened by China?", we can answer with a qualified "no." Although Southeast Asian troubles are increased by Chinese support for communist insurgencies, the real threat of these rebellions is a function of internal rather than of external forces. Beyond this, insofar as there is Chinese influence affecting the decisions of local governments, particularly in foreign affairs, it is rooted in the basic power relations of Asia and not subject to decisive, long-term change by outside interference.

If the Chinese threat to Southeast Asia is marginal, so too are United States interests in the area. Space precludes detailed discussion of this basic point, but the "worst case" argument must be answered at least in summary, lest rejection of our "China threat" analysis leads to automatic acceptance of the proposition that vital United States interests are thereby threatened. First, the "domino theory" states that all Southeast Asian regimes are vulnerable to Communist insurgency and that victory in one country will somehow spill over into neighboring areas. But as we have already seen, these societies vary greatly in their capacity to cope with insurgency. Twenty years of experience should disabuse both local rebels and foreign "viewers with alarm" from simplistic "trend" or "wave of the future" projections, regardless of how the Vietnam war ends.

Second, even should China become emboldened by its growing strength and change its policy so drastically as to cow governments into submission, either through satellite insurgencies or by direct military pressure, control over the region's resources would neither solve Peking's basic developmental problems nor transform China from a second to a first class power. Nor would extension of hostile control over the Strait of Malacca inflict irreparable harm to the commercial and military communications of Japan and the United States, since alternative sea routes are available.[17] Reference to Japan raises the bogus analogy of World War II, when United States interests appeared sufficiently threatened by Tokyo's takeover of Indo-China to move us onto a collision course. Aside from the lack of comparable resource dependence today, alternatives to tin and rubber long since obviating such need, Japan's maritime power has no counterpart in China. For Peking to extend its domination much beyond the mainland, an entire navy would have to be developed, China's largest ships at present being only destroyers. To be sure, its growing submarine fleet can harass shipping lanes; but without supporting air and sea strength such an operation would be short-lived at best. Thus with or without Southeast Asia, China's conventional power poses no foreseeable threat to the security of Japan, the Philippines, Indonesia, Australia, and New Zealand, much less to the interests of the United States in the West and Southwest Pacific.

Exempted from this analysis, of course, are China's thermonuclear weapons. Peking's present TU-16 bomber fleet and imminent IRBM's will provide a capability of striking key targets in the arc of Asia from Japan to India, most of which lie within a thousand miles of mainland launch points. However, this takes us into entirely separate questions of Chinese vulnerability and sensitivity to American retaliatory capabilities. As I have elaborated elsewhere in some detail, our deterrence which has sufficed for the Soviet Union should more than suffice for China, given China's greatly inferior defensive and retaliatory capability.[18] The prudence and self-restraint which has marked

17. Bundy, op. cit., argues along these lines, although he differs with our general analysis in terms of the threat of China's influence transmitted through Communist insurgencies.
18. A fuller examination of assumptions and fallacies associated with projection of Chinese nuclear strategy may be found in *ABM*, edited by Abram Chayes and Jerome B. Wiesner, (New York: Harper and Row, 1969), "The Chinese Nuclear Threat" by the author.

Chinese military movement outside that country since 1949 is almost certain to dominate military thinking in Peking over the next decade or more.

To return to the question of United States interests, a third "worst case" proposition requires examination: will American commitments elsewhere in Asia and Europe remain credible to friend and foe if we reduce our commitments in Southeast Asia and Communist victories should follow? This is an exceedingly difficult question, involving as it does the perspectives of various elites which view United States behavior in the West Pacific, in NATO, and at home. Our only available evidence is inferential but powerful, namely these elites' responses to the Indo-China war. At best—excepting Australia and New Zealand—they have been bribed to contribute troops, as with South Korea and Thailand. At worst, they have defaulted on their implied SEATO obligations, as with Britain and Pakistan, or been openly critical, as with France. In between these extremes stand the majority who remain mute or whispering critics, hoping that America will withdraw soon enough to recover the self-confidence necessary to sustain the material cost and human sacrifice of possible future tests elsewhere. Certainly, few Asian and no European allies publicly admit to the "credibility of commitment" linkage we profess is at stake.

Thus, when all the arguments are reduced to their essentials, only one "vital" United States interest remains at stake in Southeast Asia: our sense of ourselves. If our leadership insists our self-defined mission in the world includes victory by the Saigon generals over their opponents in the jungles and rice-paddies of South Vietnam, Cambodia, Laos, and perhaps even North Vietnam, too, then failure by those generals necessarily becomes our failure. So long as a single American pilot flies in support of Saigon's forces or a single American adviser guides their military operations, we will continue to identify our interest with theirs. By extension, this also applies to the generals and politicians in the remaining third of Laos still outside Pathet Lao control, as well as to the regime in Bangkok.

In a very real sense, the interests of Southeast Asians and Americans *are* intertwined by the deep involvement of the Pentagon and the Central Intelligence Agency in the affairs of

Laos and Thailand, wholly apart from South Vietnam. More than presidential rhetoric links Washington to Saigon, Vientiane, and Bangkok. Over a decade of effort involving thousands of Americans and billions of dollars has built up massive bureaucratic interests whose leverage on United States policy clearly outweighs dissenting views in the State Department and the Congress. As congressional hearings have shown, the visible implementers of policy in Washington and in the field resemble the proverbial tip of the iceberg in proportion to the invisible proponents and implementers.[19] It is tempting to pit Henry Kissinger against Secretary Rogers in crediting United States policy with success or failure. But the policy process is determined by institutions far more than by individuals. It is the identity of interests between the Department of Defense and CIA operations, on the one hand, and various Southeast Asian regimes, armies, and factions on the other hand, which is subsumed under the president's euphemism "our interests and those of the Free World in Southeast Asia."

This does not mean we have *no* interests in Southeast Asia. On the contrary, United States interests there, as elsewhere, range from private investment to public concern with the welfare of our fellow men. We would like to promote trade and commerce that is profitable for Americans and Asians. We would like to improve living standards through assisting developments such as the Mekong River Project. We prefer peace to war and have an interest in reducing regional frictions and improving regional security through such institutions as the Association of Southeast Asian Nations (ASEAN). To equate a reduction of American military commitments and elimination of American military and subversive involvement with the "isolationism" of the 1930s is innocent ignorance at best and a calculated deceit at worst. No one familiar with the extensive American involvement in Asia can possibly believe that removal

19. U. S., Congress, Senate, Subcommittee on United States Security Agreements and Commitments of the Committee on Foreign Relations, *United States Security Agreements and Commitments Abroad*, 91st Cong., vols. I and II. Despite heavy deletions, Part 2, "The Kingdom of Laos," illustrates the problem of discerning policy and commitments from the official, visible activity in a particular country.

of our bases from the area totally abandons Asians to their own resources.[20]

V. United States Illusions

In short, we do have other alternatives between Fortress America and Pax Americana. Both concepts are illusions, devoid of reality and dangerous to practice. We fought two world wars in denial of Fortress America. It is dead, never to be resurrected. We have fought two Asian wars in pursuit of Pax Americana. This illusion is dying slowly, taking with it the lives of hundreds of thousands of Asians and Americans. But if the determined resistance of North Vietnam to our military might signifies anything, it most assuredly is the end of Pax Americana as a viable policy in Southeast Asia.

This is not the only illusion that must be abandoned if we are to have policy goals consonant with the means available to us as defined by our own institutions and values. In the final analysis, these institutions and values are all that hold us together as a society. Without them, we will either be united in a garrison state with total repression and regulation, or divided into warring factions, each fighting for his own. This does not mean we must promote these institutions and values through our foreign policy, modeling other societies on our own. But it does mean that we must live by them to the extent possible or they shall die of disbelief.

One such value is the freedom for each society to make its own way of life, whether in isolation or involvement, in revolution or in religion, in anarchy or autocracy. Perhaps no more insidious phrase masks the iniquities of American imperialism than "nation-building." Behind this benign image of social engineers constructing a new order throughout the world lies a persistent effort to shape the future for other peoples by exploiting our political, economic, and military ascendancy in various areas. The fact of the matter is that we cannot build a total political system in any culture other than our own, and we still have

20. One of the most cogent and concise analyses of United States "interests" in Southeast Asia is offered by Gurtov, *Southeast Asia Tomorrow*, op. cit. Bundy, op. cit., has a surprising degree of agreement with Gurtov, considering Bundy's role as assistant secretary of state for Far East affairs, 1964-9.

much to do here at home. Elsewhere we lack the knowledge, the language, and the access necessary to create viable and lasting leadership, institutions, and customs, all of which combine with ideology to form political systems.

In this regard, our failure in South Vietnam should have been seen as a foregone conclusion. This failure is a function of wrong goals, not merely wrong means. From 1954 to the present, we have persisted in the illusion we could "build a nation."[21] The illusion was enhanced by the characteristic American confusion of individuals with institutions. Here at home, we focus on the mayor, the governor, and the president as embodiments of our political system and hold them accountable for its successes or failures. We continuously change them in a vain search for improvement, refusing to recognize that various components of the system must be changed or nothing will really be different. It is these components which constrain the power to tax and to police, the distribution of rewards and the allocation of resources. So, too, abroad we personify politics, identifying with personalities and ignoring their power base (or absence thereof) as well as that of their opponents. In China we "stuck" with an individual, Chiang Kai-shek, despite the fact that only Mao Tse-tung had a viable political system, as well as a comprehensive, dynamic ideology which meshed with a powerful organizational ability and mobilization appeals.[22] Again in South Vietnam we chose to "sink or swim with Ngo Dinh Diem," despite his inability to abandon a personal mandarinate dominated by psychotic relatives. We personified power that Diem simply did not have as an ideology or a political system.

To be sure, unlike Chiang, Diem did not face a charismatic competitor in the NLF and Ho was a background competitor. Moreover, in contrast with the Chinese Communist party, the National Liberation Front had too much terror and too little revolutionary appeal to generate sufficient support from such key socio-economic groups as students, intellectuals, and peas-

21. In addition to Cooper, op. cit., see Roger Hilsman, *To Move a Nation* (Garden City, N.Y.: Doubleday & Co., 1967).

22. A brilliantly insightful account of the China fiasco with strong parallels anticipating later United States policy in South Vietnam may be found in Barbara Tuchman, *Stillwell and the American Experience in China, 1911-1946* (New York: Macmillan Co., 1971).

ants. These two weaknesses kept the NLF from winning all South Vietnam before the intervention of massive American military air and ground power could stem the tide. But the NLF success was great enough to require the smashing of its political system by total war involving every type of ordinance in the American inventory, excepting bacteriological and nuclear weapons. A vast array of crippling and lethal anti-personnel devices, ranging from white phosphorous and napalm to "bomblets" which fill the air with tiny steel pellets, rained indiscriminately on combatant and non-combatant alike from ubiquitous aircraft, artillery, and mortars. B-52's showered millions of tons of bombs. Defoliants denuded trees and destroyed crops. Yet in February 1968, three years after regular United States troops entered combat, the Communists could still launch simultaneous surprise attacks against a score of towns and storm into Hue and Saigon, without any prior warning from the civilian populace.

Four years have passed since the 1968 Tet offensive. By most evidence, we have smashed enough of the Communist political system or "infrastructure" to prevent any similar occurrence in the near future. We have done this by adopting his means of penetrating the society with intelligence agents, terrorizing and bribing informers, assassinating "the enemy," and "securing" the surrounding countryside through American firepower and South Vietnamese manpower. But is this enough? Authoritative reports in Washington claim tens of thousands remain loyal to the NLF throughout the central and provincial apparatus. Our bombs and bullets can destroy enemy sanctuaries in Cambodia and Laos. But they cannot destroy enemy appeals in South Vietnam until a viable indigenous political system can competitively command the voluntary loyalty of its inhabitants as an independent regime, free of American control and direction.

President Nixon declares that United States policy is to enable the South Vietnamese to "stand on their own feet" and "decide their own future." If this really means the assured survival of the present Saigon regime, we will never leave South Vietnam and our interests will remain tied to our illusions. If, however, we genuinely wish the Vietnamese to decide for themselves their own political system and their own future, then we must leave immediately. After seventeen years of economic assistance, political direction, and provision for a million men under arms, this society has absorbed virtually all the American "aid" it can take. Now is the time to go its own way, before our illusions and theirs tempt its leadership into greater military adventures.

For it is our illusion that what are inextricably political-military problems can be "fixed" by purely military means. Prince Sihanouk's delicate balancing act brought him down in a mad moment of mutual miscalculation between the prince and his critics in Phnom Penh. It mattered little that he represented the only symbolic cement in a fragile but viable political system. American military frustration over years of Communist sanctuary in eastern Cambodia exploded with an invasion aimed at wiping out Communist strongholds. This move won political concurrence in Washington where refusal to risk the possible downfall of Lon Nol once again identified American interests with a personality, not with a viable political system. True, the sanctuary disappeared; the strongholds were smashed. But the Communists still control a third of Cambodia, and the combination of South Vietnamese manpower and United States airpower continues to ravage much of the country. Another political system awaits rebuilding.

In the Laos invasion of 1971, once again the illusion of a "quick fix" and a "last blow" substituted countless casualties for a political solution to the conflicting aims of Hanoi and Washington. After ten years of secret warfare behind the screen of a fictional state that was little more than the cover for battle between proxy armies, we decided to end the fiction and to "cut the Ho Chi Minh trail." Saigon's callous disregard for its own forces appears to match Washington's view that so long as the casualties are not American, the war can be pursued indefinitely. After two years in office, President Nixon finally conceded that an indefinite war was Hanoi's prerogative should it choose to fight on rather than submit to our demands at Paris.[23]

There are those, of course, who argue that the war could have been ended at any time if we chose to invade North Vietnam. Against this position, I hold that any prospect of success in such a move would bring Peking actively into the war. We do not need to take Hanoi's explicit warnings at face value nor do we need to rely on interpretations of Peking's more ambiguous

23. President Richard M. Nixon, op. cit.

pledges. We need only recall Chinese intervention in the Korean War, at a time when that country had just emerged from two decades of civil war and foreign invasion and lacked any modern military power, to know Peking would not abandon Hanoi to defeat on North Vietnamese soil. Washington thought the Chinese were "bluffing" in 1950 when they warned us against crossing the thirty-eighth parallel.[24] Three months later thousands of dead and wounded Marines provided grim testimony to the contrary.

This is the true "Chinese threat"—and one we must heed. President Kennedy considered sending American troops into Laos in 1961. Chinese forces moved into the two northern provinces adjoining China's borders, where they have remained ever since.[25] Washington got the word and moved to Geneva instead of to a larger war. In 1965, President Johnson escalated the air war to North Vietnam and moved massive American ground forces to South Vietnam. This time Chinese army units entered North Vietnam, complete with regular uniforms and military communications which they knew would identify them to United States intelligence as the People's Liberation Army. Included in the fifty thousand Chinese troops stationed in North Vietnam from 1965 to 1968 were two anti-aircraft divisions whose regular exchanges of fire with attacking American aircraft drew casualties on both sides. When our bombing stopped, the troops went back across the border but they can return at any time Hanoi and Peking find it necessary.

These are the "moments of truth" for any policy which seeks to "contain China." Either we are willing to fight or we must abandon situations that threaten China's direct military involvement. There is no ignominy in avoiding war that results from over-commitment. Khrushchev did just this in the Cuban missile crisis, without destroying the credibility of Russian reaction to revolt or invasion in East Europe. And for those who argue an alternative course lies with nuclear weapons against Chinese manpower, one can only submit them to endless viewing of the

24. Allen S. Whiting, *China Crosses the Yalu* (Stanford, Cal.: Stanford University Press, 1967).
25. Hilsman, op. cit.

Hiroshima and Nagasaki films and hope that their vicarious nightmares of suffering suffice to prevent revisiting mankind with that horrible reality.[26]

VI.   Prescription for the Future

It should be clear by now that there is no "quick fix" or pat formula to achieve United States goals in Southeast Asia. Indeed, those goals as conventionally stated appear unattainable by any means, most certainly if those means are dictated by Washington against the will of peoples in the area. We seek "peace with honor" but pursue this by the most dishonorable war in our history. The peoples of the area, whether Burmese, Thai, Cambodian, or Vietnamese, also pursue "peace with honor." However, their definition of "peace" is relative and can tolerate local insurgency as a preferable burden to American domination and destruction via "counterinsurgency." Moreover, their sense of "honor" permits their bending like the bamboo before the winds from Peking, rather than being grafted onto the American oak. In short, ideal goals of absolute peace and total independence must always be compromised, given the realities of international relations. The compromises historically adopted by the peoples of Southeast Asia dismay our tidy sense of firmness, resolve, and clarity, dressed up in legalistic or journalistic formulas. But the alternative is perpetuating the area's agony as a cockpit for conflict between the ideologies of capitalism and communism as reflected in the power pretensions of the United States and China.

We cannot, therefore, look for successful "solutions," least of all those stamped "Made in America." Neither the prescription of "neutralization" nor the institutionalization of "regional security" carries any serious promise of achieving United States goals of preventing the spread of communism and the influence

26. A critical examination of this matter and the role nuclear weapons might play is offered by Earl C. Ravenal, "The Nixon Doctrine and Our Asian Commitments," *Foreign Affairs* (January 1971). Ravenal was director of the Asian Division (Systems Analysis) in the Office of the Secretary of Defense, 1967-69. Former Secretary of State Dean Rusk has said he could not "imagine a war with mainland China that would not be nuclear," NBC television interview, 3 July 1971.

of China in Southeast Asia.[27] We can negotiate limited agreements which arrange for the exclusion of foreign troops and bases, specifically those of Washington and Peking. But we cannot negotiate the removal of "outside interference in the internal affairs" of these countries because neither we nor the Chinese are able to divest ourselves of the "power complex" which compels us to exert our various diplomatic, economic, and subversive skills at influencing other governments to do as we wish. We believe in American investments abroad, for instance, just as the Chinese believe in revolutions abroad. We believe our democratic doctrines, United States capital, and trade help others as well as ourselves. The Chinese believe the same for their revolutionary doctrines, their aid, and trade. Thus each government will seek to protect and advance its interests at the expense of the other.

Fortunately, Peking's record of self-restraint over the past twenty-one years provides one basis for hope that this competition can be limited to relatively peaceful means. Another basis for optimism is the fact that, with the exception of Laos, there is no "power vacuum" in the area. Laos is a legal fiction, created by the 1954 Geneva Accords. It lacks the cohesive core of traditional interrelationships that provide the minimum basis for a sense of nationhood. Burma most closely approximates this crisis of identity. But elsewhere indigenous elements dominate sufficiently to give solid support to central governments with pervasive political systems. Capture or transformation of that system is, in our vernacular, the "name of the game." Once we recognize these two facts—Chinese restraint and local strength— a third basis for optimism concerning the future of Southeast Asia can emerge: growing American restraint. Some may say we already exercise restraint since we have not used nuclear weapons, destroyed the dikes of North Vietnam, or obliterated Hanoi. But the fact remains that it is only Chinese weapons, and not

27. One of the more thoughtful and detailed examinations of various alternatives may be found in Bernard K. Gordon, *Toward Disengagement in Asia* (Englewood Cliffs, N.J.: Prentice-Hall, Inc., 1969). The attraction of "neutralization" as a concept is reflected in its recurring advocacy by statesmen of such widely differing viewpoints as Chester Bowles in 1960, General Charles de Gaulle in 1963, and William P. Bundy in 1971.

Chinese pilots and troops, which enable Communist forces throughout Indo-China to withstand the unprecedented barrage of bombs and bullets fired by American pilots together with the United States-supported South Vietnamese army and air force. Not until all such American combat in the air as well as on the ground stops can we begin to speak of our restraint.

But beyond this minimal measure we must remove the American military bases which commit us to the defense of a particular government regardless of the threat it faces, if its overthrow in turn threatens those bases. Instead of the bases being means to an end, they become ends in themselves, necessitating our involvement in the internal affairs of the host society as well as making us hostage to that government's survival. The physical pressures of United States troops and bases does produce a (high) degree of "credibility" for our commitments abroad. But if air, naval, and ultimately our missile strength is incapable of convincing a particular government we mean to abide by whatever commitments we have undertaken on its behalf, then we must ask: how solid is our relationship? If it is so fraught with mistrust, perhaps we should avoid the costs of commitment altogether.

This does not mean abstention from assisting genuine efforts, whether bilateral or multilateral, to improve the political, economic, and military capabilities of Southeast Asian countries. We have considerable room for improving our relations with the Colombo Plan countries, and the Association of Southeast Asian Nations (ASEAN) holds more promise than any of its antecedents. The Asian Development Bank and the World Bank are alternatives to American economic assistance, as is Japan, of course. And once the People's Republic of China is in the United Nations, we can hope for it to share the consultative, guidance, and assistance roles of United Nation agencies, most particularly in the Economic Commission for Asia and the Far East (ECAFE).

These are modest, fumbling, and inadequate efforts, at best. However, they appear far closer to the will and the capacity of Southeast Asian governments desirous of strengthening their independence against external pressures than any massive, overarching American design for the area. Indeed, in one sense the very concept of Southeast Asia as an "area" in the politico-military sense is an American myth, born in the bureaucratic administering of World War II and sustained by the captious language of postwar writers and officials. Calling it a "region" does not make it one, except perhaps in the purely geographic sense. And, ironically, if it is the geographic meaning that justifies the term, we are implicitly acknowledging by the term "Southeast" that "Asia's" center must be China.

Whether by this irony or by more direct logic, then, a United States policy toward Southeast Asia has not been and cannot be separated from our policy toward China. That, of course, is an entire subject in itself. However, we must at least consider in closing whether we mean to face the People's Republic as a parental guardian at best and a policeman at worst, curbing its instincts and its behavior by all the means available. Or do we genuinely seek to normalize our relations with Peking, dismantling our heritage of involvement in the Chinese Civil War and the Korean War so as to eliminate as much as possible the chance of nuclear conflict in Asia? Are we to circle, with nuclear daggers drawn, around the Korean and Southeast Asian peninsulas, not to mention the offshore islands in the Taiwan Strait? Or will we systematically attempt to defuse our confrontation, even if it means painful compromises with our assumptions of American ascendancy in Asia?

If thirty-five thousand Americans died in Korea, at least ten times that many Chinese perished there. If we are willing to support Saigon indefinitely, so too is Peking willing to back Hanoi. Of course, we cannot be certain that peace and security in Asia can be obtained through Peking's "Five Principles of Peaceful Coexistence." This uncertainty, however, is inherent in all diplomacy and it is our obligation to remove it, one way or the other, by utilizing all of our resources and initiative in negotiating with the People's Republic of China. However much "peace" as an idealized concept may be unattainable, to the degree it can be approximated at all in Asia, peace will ultimately be secured only with the active participation of the authorities in Peking in security arrangements that have mutual interests to reinforce their legal language. These arrangements may be formal and informal, explicit and tacit, openly and secretly communicated.

However, their possibility in the near future is greater than at any time in the past, lending hope for the transformation of Sino-American relations from total confrontation to peaceful competition.

The Obsolescence of United States Foreign Policy

Hans J. Morgenthau

THE VIETNAM ISSUE and the tragedy in which in different ways this issue has involved all of us cannot be justly considered in isolation from the overall character of American foreign policy. There was a time when I thought—and quite wrongly—that if one could only get to President Johnson and explain to him the issue, he would see the light and not take a further step forward. This was, as I can see now in retrospect, a wrong and in a sense a naïve assumption. For the commitment to a meritless venture, to a venture which is without merit not only politically and militarily but, more particularly, morally, this commitment cannot be put at the doorstep of a particular president or a particular secretary of state or a particular administration. In a very profound sense it is the result of a wrong way of thinking about foreign policy. And so it is only when we look at American foreign policy in general as an overall structure of thought and action that we can understand this otherwise strange and incomprehensible persistence in error which has characterized our intervention in Indo-China.

If one wants to define what is wrong with American foreign policy in one simple statement, I think one can say that it is obsolete. There exists today a chasm between the way we are thinking about and acting on foreign policy, on the one hand, and the objective conditions of our existence, on the other. When the present foreign policy of the United States was first conceived and put into action in the famous fifteen weeks of the spring of 1947 in the form of the policy of containment, the Truman Doctrine, the Marshall Plan, these great innovative policies were all admirably appropriate to the issues which we were facing then. Our reaction to those issues in the form of those three foreign policies testifies to the creativity and courage of the people who conceived them.

In a sense, however, it has been the very success of those policies which has become the curse of American foreign policy. For because the policy of containment was successful in Europe, we thought we could erect it into a universal principle of statecraft and apply it elsewhere, anywhere, without any limitations of time and space. The issue which we were facing in the aftermath of the Second World War in Europe was the conventional one of a powerful and locally irresistible army standing in the heart of Europe, one hundred miles east of the Rhine, with no counterforce to the west to contain it. Thus it was almost a foregone conclusion—it was in any case an absolute necessity dictated by the national interest—somehow to counteract the presence of that army through the policy of containment.

However, what was possible and eminently successful in Europe proved to be unsuccessful and even impossible elsewhere. It proved so in particular in Southeast Asia and in Asia in general. For the mechanical projection of our modes of thought and action from Europe to Asia showed that we were completely unaware of the profound distinction between the issues which we were facing in Asia as over against the issues which had been dealt with successfully in Europe. In Asia we were not facing an army poised to sweep in a conventional way over frontiers. The idea that Mao Tse-tung is a successor of Hitler and that the Chinese armies are poised to sweep over Asia like the hordes of Genghis Khan has been an obsession with some of our policy-makers, who found there empirical proof for the limitless expansionism of communism; but it has no equivalent in actual reality.

Chinese power and influence are not likely to expand through the conventional means of conquering armies. What impresses anybody who has traveled in Asia with his eyes and ears open is the enormous impact which the renaissance of China has made throughout Asia from Tokyo to Karachi. This is the great secular event in the recent history of Asia: for the first time in more than a hundred years this colossus, which by its very existence for millenia dominated the cultural and political life of Asia, all of a sudden is in the process of coming into its own again. The Chinese have not used for centuries what they would call the crude western methods of physical conquest in order to expand their empire. They have relied upon the enormous power and attractiveness of their culture, of their very existence, one might say, because what is so inescapable in Asia and which one only feels when one lives in Asia is exactly the presence of between 700 and 800 million people, intelligent, industrious, and the heirs of an old and magnificent civilization. So the influence which the Chinese have exerted in Asia and which they are beginning to exert again is an extremely subtle, intangible, psychological, cultural influence which cannot be staved off with armies equipped with the modern paraphernalia of warfare. In other words, if we want to contain China, we cannot use the military means which we have been trying to use.

I should also say that it is not only that the means which we have been trying to use are inappropriate to the issue, but it is also that although the Chinese have frequently talked like madmen, they have acted for twenty years with great circumspection on the chessboard of foreign policy. If one looks at what the Chinese have actually done or aspired to—Taiwan, the offshore islands, Tibet, the rectification of the McMahon line as the frontier between India and China, the intervention in the Korean War when we approached the Yalu—all those steps have nothing to do with limitless expansionism, Communist or non-Communist inspired. But they have everything to do with the traditional national aspirations of China. Thus it is not by accident that those moves of Mao Tse-tung in foreign policy which I have just mentioned have been applauded either openly or surreptitiously by Chiang Kai-shek. Mao Tse-tung and Chiang Kai-shek see perfectly eye to eye when it comes to the issue of Taiwan. They both claim that Taiwan is an integral part of China, but happen to disagree as to who shall govern China. And Chiang Kai-shek had in his cabinet a commissioner for Tibet and Outer Mongolia, implying that those territories, too, are integral parts of the Chinese empire.

So, one of the fundamental mistakes we have made in Asia is to look at Asia from the perspective of Europe and, more particularly, from the perspective of our successes in Europe. Because containment was so successful in Europe, we thought the same kind of containment would be successful in Asia. But aside from the fact that the nature of the Chinese threat, such as it is, is entirely different from what the Soviet threat has been in Europe, there is really nothing to contain in the traditional sense. In other words, the predominance of China on the Asian mainland is a fact of life, as the predominance of the United States in the Western Hemisphere is a fact of life: both are existential. If we cannot accommodate ourselves to the predominance of China in Asia, we have to get rid of China—quite a task, which the Japanese had no success in performing. In other words, there is, one might almost say, a madness in our approach to the Asian problems in that we completely misunderstand the nature of those problems and are trying to solve them with methods which are completely inappropriate, which have really no relation to the issues at hand. If we look at the utter futility of what we have been doing in Vietnam, the senseless destruction of men and things, and ask ourselves, "Why? Why have decent and fairly intelligent men embarked persistently upon such an insane and morally repulsive course of action?", we are forced to admit that what is in good measure responsible for this madness is a complete lack of understanding of the actual situation in Asia, of our interests with regard to that situation, of the power which we are capable of bringing to bear upon it.

The second fundamental weakness of our foreign policy, which again has come to the fore in Indo-China, is our fundamental misunderstanding of the relationship between communism and the foreign policies of communist governments. There was a time, in the 1940s and 1950s, when one could maintain the proposition that we had to contain all communist movements and governments throughout the world without distinction because they were all under the control and at the service of the Soviet Union. Since we were committed to the containment of the Soviet Union, we were *a fortiori* also committed to the containment of communism *per se*. Whatever the merits of this position might have been twenty-five years ago, it has no merit today.

Communism has transformed itself from a monolith, dominated and controlled by the Soviet Union, into a polycentric agglomeration of different communist movements and governments, all pursuing what they regard to be their particular national interests. To say, as a former secretary of state used to say frequently, "We are in Vietnam to stop Communism," is an entirely misplaced generalization. For one has first to ask, under present conditions, what kind of communism is it we want to contain? Is this a communism subservient to Russia? Is this a communism subservient to China? Is it a communism straddling the fence between the two major communist powers, such as the communism of Rumania? Or is it a communism like that of Yugoslavia; that is to say, a strictly nationalistic communism without close ties to the world-communist movement? And once that issue is settled, we have to ask ourselves what is the bearing of this particular type of communism upon the interests of the United States? Then we can start devising an American foreign policy with regard to that communism.

But this we have never done in Southeast Asia, nor have we done it consistently elsewhere. We have taken it for granted, and the men who make our foreign policy still take it for granted, that our main objective in Vietnam is to keep the communists out of Saigon. Now I would rather see the communists out of Saigon than in it, but I would still maintain that this objective is not worth the life of a single American soldier; for the vital interests of the United States are not involved. It is certainly preferable from a moral or political or, one might say, philosophic point of view to have as few communist governments as possible. But we will see elsewhere in the world communist or pro-communist governments coming to power, and we will have to accommodate ourselves to that undesirable fact. So the simple equation of communism with an evil which we have to oppose as a sacred mission we must perform is a second root of the disaster which we are facing in Vietnam and which we are likely to face elsewhere if we do not change our modes of thought and action.

Thirdly, we have assumed, again on the basis of our experiences in Europe, more particularly with the Marshall Plan, that our wealth and technological know-how qualify us to transform the so-called underdeveloped world in the image of our own technological civilization. Thus many of our people have gone into Vietnam with great enthusiasm, with a pure heart, with idealistic intentions, only to bring about terrible misery, death, and disaster. For they completely misunderstood the limits of our power in the political, military, and economic fields. I have heard it said by very intelligent and highly-placed people, when I asked them why we are in Vietnam, "We are there in order to help the Vietnamese in nation-building." And we are flattered by the thought that we are some kind of universal architect of nations. Other peoples do not know how to build nations. We know, and we help them build them.

In truth, of course, there have been in Vietnam social entities with the characteristics which we attribute to nations long before Columbus discovered America. What we have done in Vietnam in the process of trying to build a nation in our image is to utterly destroy the nation's social fabric which had existed there for millenia. Our experience in Vietnam justifies a general observation about the dangers of political actions that stem from the goodness of heart but are unenlightened by understanding and knowledge. I remember a statement by the English writer Henry Taylor: "It sometimes happens that he who would not hurt a fly will hurt a nation." Many of our people who have gone to Vietnam inspired by a typical American idealism have, indeed, perhaps not harmed a fly; but they have contributed to the ruin of a nation.

There is in this conception that our wealth and our technological capabilities give us a kind of divine mission to aid the rest of the world a good-hearted but naïve ethnocentrism or culturecentrism. For where is it written that, first of all, the nations which we call underdeveloped are really underdeveloped in terms of certain objective standards? What do we mean by saying that Vietnam or China are underdeveloped nations? What we mean to say is that those nations do not have the same kind of economic productivity and technological know-how we have. But it is nowhere written in any sacred or non-sacred scriptures I can think of that all nations must aspire, by dint of a universal law, to the same kind of industrial society, GNP, and technology of which we used to be so proud. Even we have not been so proud of these achievements recently after smelling the air and trying to drink the water, saturated with the by-products of these achievements.

But even if this were not so, there is an utter naïvété in the idea that all nations are disadvantaged and underdeveloped which do not measure up to our American standards. I remember about ten years ago I met the former head of our foreign aid mission in Burma who had been there for three years and came back utterly discouraged and disenchanted. He said, "How can you bring about economic development in a nation which believes that success in this world is a handicap for that success in another world which is the only success that really counts?" I am not prepared to say that we are right and the Burmese are wrong, or vice versa. I am only raising a fundamental moral question about the admissibility of a naïve ethnocentrism which believes that our values are universal and that anybody who has different values, and therefore falls short of ours, must be brought up with fire and sword, if necessary, to our standards. Aside from the fact that it does not work, there are some philosophic and moral defects in this proposition.

That brings me to still another point—again, all these points are interconnected—and that is the assumption that certain nations are underdeveloped, they do not measure up to our productivity and our technology, because they are poor, their problem being simply economic; give them money, give them technological know-how, and they will pull themselves up and be on the road to economic development. What we have not understood are two factors which stand in the way of economic development in many underdeveloped nations and which have absolutely nothing to do with relative poverty.

One is the fact, to which I have already referred with regard to Burma, that certain cultures simply adhere to values which are incompatible with economic development. Nations which belong to such cultures have simply to make up their minds and make a choice. They cannot have it both ways. They cannot maintain their ancient values and at the same time embark on economic development. Take, for instance, so seemingly simple and obvious a value as saving, saving for an emergency or saving for profitable investment. There are hundreds of millions of people living at this moment who have no conception of saving, for whom this conception is completely incomprehensible. A few years ago we gave some motorized fishing boats to Kenya which has large fishing grounds that are uneconomically exploited. What did the Kenyan fishermen do? After they had gotten their usual catch, say, in five hours rather than ten, they stopped fishing. They lived in a static world from which the very conception of economic progress was absent. No amount of American dollars, no amount of American goodwill is going to transform the cultural outlook of those fishermen in such a way as to put them on the road to economic development. If they cannot do it from within without foreign aid, as the Japanese have done since they emerged from isolation and feudalism more than a century ago, they will not do it at all.

Even more important is the other factor which we have tended to overlook and which is likely to be one of the crucial factors in our future foreign policy: the political factor. We assume that some people are poor and underdeveloped because they have insufficient natural resources. In truth, however, many underdeveloped nations, rich in natural resources, are under-developed because they are governed by elites with a vested interest in economic underdevelopment. Take the problem of illiteracy. We assume that in some countries 90 percent of the population are illiterate because those poor governments do not have enough money to build schools, to train and pay teachers, to buy books, and so forth. No doubt, there are governments thus deprived. But we should not forget that throughout human history artificially maintained illiteracy has been a potent political weapon. It is not by accident that in the states of the Confederacy teaching the slaves how to read and write was prohibited by law, for illiterate slaves are more easily governed. And the peasant of northeastern Brazil who cannot read or write is less of a revolutionary danger than the one who can.

Much of economic backwardness is the result of natural deficiencies to be remedied by foreign aid. For example, looking simply at the objective resources of Brazil, it is clear that Brazil could be as prosperous and powerful a nation as the United States is. In terms of the extent of its territory, the quality and quantity of natural resources, and its climate, it is not dissimilar. Certainly, Brazil is not naturally disadvantaged to any considerable degree in comparison with the United States. Why, then, is it that Brazil is a third-rate power? Why is it that the masses of Brazil are poor? Not because Brazil is lacking in natural resources, but because it is lacking in a political system, in a social system, in a government which has the will to bring about economic development.

Take another simple example: land reform in South Vietnam. Since 1954, we have urged land reform upon a succession of South Vietnamese governments, and a succession of South Vietnamese governments has adopted legislation calling for land reform. Nothing has happened for the very simple reason that one of the main social, economic, and political supports of that succession of South Vietnamese governments is centered in the absentee landlords who have a vital interest in preventing land reform. So any South Vietnamese government which would start land reform in earnest would destroy the very social and economic base of its political power. It would commit political suicide. This we cannot expect.

It is this expectation that is at the root of the failure of the Alliance for Progress designed to start Latin America on the road to economic development. We tried to foster radical economic and social and, in consequence, also political change through the instrumentality of governments which in most instances were, and in view of their political interests had to be, either indifferent or hostile to that change. Foreign aid, conceived in such apolitical terms, has proven to be not only useless as an instrument for bringing about economic development, but also counterproductive. For channeling foreign aid through elites having a stake in the preservation of the *status quo* strengthened the very *status quo* we intended to transform. In many countries which were the recipients of massive American foreign aid, the poor stayed as poor as they had been before, and the rich became richer with the aid they received from the United States. Thus the gap between the rich and the poor which foreign aid was supposed to narrow, if not to close, was actually widened by foreign aid apolitically conceived.

Thus, a few exceptions to the contrary notwithstanding, foreign aid has been a failure. For different reasons it has been a failure for the Russians and for the Chinese as well. As a result, this three-cornered competition in what we used to call the struggle for the minds of the underdeveloped world has largely ended. All three of us now give foreign aid on a pragmatic, limited basis. Since we have come to recognize that most underdeveloped nations prefer to be miserable in their own way to being happy in the American, Chinese, or Russian way, we are restraining our reformatory impulses and are instead making our own political interests the ultimate standard for determining the quantity and quality of our foreign aid. The United States giving military aid to Greece, China building a railroad for Tanzania, the Soviet Union giving economic and military aid to Egypt are cases in point.

Yet, while the social, economic, and political ills which foreign aid was supposed to cure have remained unattended, they have continued to exert an ever-increasing destructive effect upon the *status quo*. Or, to put it bluntly, many of the underdeveloped nations throughout the world, especially in Latin America, are in a revolutionary or prerevolutionary state. In many of these countries the choice is not between revolution and the *status quo*, but between one kind of revolution and another kind of revolution. Revolution itself is likely to be inevitable. It is interesting to note that a large and increasingly powerful segment of the Catholic Church in Latin America, the so-called Third World wing, is fully aware of this fact. In Brazil, in Argentina, in Colombia, and elsewhere we find young priests and even bishops and archbishops, like Archbishop Helder of Recife in Brazil, in the forefront of those movements of radical reform, if not revolution. I remember long ago I bought a copy of *Ecclesia*, the official paper of the Archdiocese of Madrid in Spain—the only paper which was not censored then—which carried an editorial arguing that revolution was inevitable, that the Evangiles are a revolutionary document, and that if Christians did not put themselves at the head of the inevitable revolution, the Communists would.

I mention this to show the utter backwardness, the utter unreality of our attitude toward revolution throughout the world. We still cling, however hesitatingly and desperately, to the outworn proposition that revolutions are Communist-inspired and therefore bad, and that we have a holy mission to protect the *status quo* against revolution. It is, of course, obvious that this is a recipe for failure. For we are simply putting ourselves on the wrong side of history. We are doing the same thing that Metternich of Austria did between 1815 and 1848 when he made it the main point of his foreign policy to prevent liberal revolutions until a liberal revolution put an end to his rule. The ever-increasing lack of influence which we are experiencing in the underdeveloped countries of Latin America and Africa is the result of our having bet and continuing to bet on the wrong horse, the horse which is bound to lose.

It is obvious here again that what we are dealing with is not primarily the weaknesses of a particular man or a particular administration. What we are dealing with is a concept of the world which is incorrect, which is mistaken in view of the actual, the existential nature of the world. In consequence, such a concept must lead to either unsuccessful or disastrous action.

Beyond these errors in our understanding of the underdeveloped world, we have been unable to come to terms with what is the most radical and the most menacing of the innovations of our age: nuclear power. Here the inadequacy and obsolescence of our modes of thought and action ought to be clear for all to see. We have not understood yet that in 1945 a new age dawned upon us, as different from the preceding one as the Middle Ages were from Antiquity, and as the Modern Age was from the Middle Ages. In consequence, the modes of thought and action which stem from the preceding age and which were largely appropriate to the issues which we had to face then are disastrously inappropriate to the issues we are facing today.

To start with a very simple and purely semantic observation: it is already an indication of the obsolescence of our thinking that we speak of nuclear weapons and nuclear war as though nuclear weapons were just weapons like machine guns or conventional bombs, and nuclear war were just another kind of war. In the concept of "weapon" and "war" there is a rationality —a relationship between a rational means used for a rational end —which is completely absent in the case of so-called nuclear weapons and nuclear war. For nuclear war or nuclear weapons are not instruments rationally used for a rational end. They are instruments of indiscriminate, total destruction. According to the calculations of the Atomic Energy Commission, fallout from a multimegaton surface nuclear explosion over Chicago could kill people walking in the streets of Buffalo. This is just one example of the unimaginable extent of the destructiveness of nuclear weapons. So even to speak and to think of nuclear weapons and nuclear war is an indication of the backwardness, of the obsolescence of our ways of thinking about the issues with which the nuclear age confronts us.

The availability of nuclear weapons has completely changed certain basic aspects of foreign and military policy which had been valid from the beginning of history to 1945. For example, the conventional arms race was a perfectly rational undertaking growing out of the balance-of-power policies of rival nations. The more machine guns a nation had as over against its competitor, the better off it was in this department. This rationality of the conventional arms race was the result of the misproportion between available weapons and possible targets. In other words, with regard to conventional weapons we lived in what one might call a military economy of scarcity.

But nuclear weapons present us with an entirely different situation: an optimum level exists beyond which it is utterly irrational to accumulate additional weapons. If one side has enough warheads to destroy its prospective enemy ten times over, even under the worst circumstances, it gains nothing by increasing its capability to the point of being able to destroy him twelve or fifteen times over. And one's enemy, who is "only" capable of destroying one six times over is, therefore, not inferior. These figures are not figments of my imagination; they represent approximately the actual distribution of nuclear power between the United States and the Soviet Union as they were estimated until recently. And as long as they were considered to be valid, we thought we were superior to the Soviet Union and the Russians were correspondingly inferior. Last year the Russians were observed to creep up on us. First, they could kill us seven times over. Then eight times. And then catastrophe loomed, they were capable of destroying us nine times over. And now, the government says, they are virtually even, or perhaps ahead of us in nuclear capability. We can "only" destroy them ten times over, but they can now perhaps destroy us eleven times over. And that is terrible. I am not trying to be funny; this is a deadly serious business. But it is very difficult not to be somewhat sarcastic when one deals with such a monumental misunderstanding, on the highest levels of government, of those simple, elementary facts of the nuclear age.

Another aspect of the same problem is the issue of defense. It has been said that every new weapon in the history of mankind has called forth a defense to counter it. Even if this statement is true with regard to conventional weapons, it is most certainly not true about nuclear weapons. Again the reason is the enormous, unimaginable destructiveness of nuclear weapons. Let me give you the two examples of area defense, the defense of cities and industrial establishments, on the one hand, and pinpoint defense, the defense of hardened missile sites, on the other. An area defense which is not 100 percent effective is not effective at all. If one side shoots down nine out of ten incoming missiles and one gets through, the defender will be as dead as if all ten had hit. Even the most enthusiastic proponents of an antiballistic-missile defense (ABM's) have not claimed more than 50 or 60 percent effectiveness. If we imagine for a moment that six out of ten incoming missiles are shot down but four get through, any of the metropolitan centers of the United States will be utterly destroyed.

Take the defense of hardened missile sites. Let us suppose we surround the missile sites in Montana and North Dakota with ABM's that have the capability to destroy incoming missiles of the magnitude of ten. The attacker need only to increase the number or destructive capability of his missiles to the magnitude of twelve and he will have saturated the defense. In other words, in a contest between attack and defense, the defense is utterly helpless because of the enormous destructiveness of nuclear weapons. But while this is obvious on logical, commonsensical grounds, we nevertheless cling to the illusion that we can defend ourselves against nuclear weapons.

This is not only an intellectual error *per se,* it is also enormously destabilizing for the nuclear equilibrium which has maintained the peace and at least a modicum of order in the world for twenty-five years. For if we sink, say, $50 billion into an ABM system, if the prestige of a whole administration and of hundreds of academics and politicians is involved in such an undertaking, we are bound to persuade ourselves in the end that this system is going to work. And once we are persuaded that it is going to work, we will no longer be as afraid of nuclear war as we were before. Imagine for a moment that during the Cuban missile crisis of 1962 Khrushchev and Kennedy had been in the possession of full-fledged ABM systems. They would certainly have been much less afraid of coming close to the nuclear abyss than they actually were, convinced that they could defend themselves against nuclear attack, that they might suffer painful, but

not unacceptable, damage. So there is an enormous danger here
that the development of defensive systems, however ineffective
they may turn out to be and however futile the undertaking may
appear to be *a priori,* will have a psychological effect upon the
policymakers on both sides which will seriously weaken, if not
destroy, the deterrent effect of nuclear weapons which thus far
has kept us alive.

I shall only say in passing that the development of ABM systems is also going to lead to an enormous increase in the number
and sophistication and efficiency of warheads designed for attack.
For since an attacker will have to be able to saturate the defensive system, he will have to create new weapons, which would not
be needed if the ABM system did not exist.

These issues raised by the existence of nuclear weapons point
to a fundamental paradox with which the foreign policy of the
United States is confronted. We have tended to believe, and we
have pursued foreign policies reflecting this belief, that the more
instruments of material power a nation possesses the greater will
be its actual power. This has proven to be a mistaken belief; we
have seen in Vietnam and in the Third World in general that
there are strict and relatively narrow limits to our power. An
unprecedented employment of material power has not been able
to subdue a primitive peasant movement in Southeast Asia, and
the resources of the richest nation on earth have not been sufficient to impress the nations of the Third World. The paradox
lies in the contrast between the enormity of the material power
available and the limited nature of the issues to be dealt with.
We have been in the position of a man armed with a sub-
machine gun who is trying to subdue a swarm of bees. This is
what I have called elsewhere "the impotence of American
power."

Finally, I have focused so far on foreign and military policy,
and perhaps if I had been considering the foreign policy of any
other country, I could stop here. But since I am speaking of the
foreign policy of the United States, I cannot stop here. For the
position of the United States in the world, the influence it has
been able to exert, the power it has been able to bring to bear,
has in good measure not been the result of its weapons, of its
army, its navy, its air force, or even the cleverness of its diplomacy. It has been the result of certain qualities of American life,

of American society, of American government, which we have offered as an example for other nations to emulate and which, what is more important, other nations have considered in the same light. This has been the source of America's greatness. This has been the ultimate source of its power and of its success.

It is obvious that this great moral and spiritual quality is, to put it mildly, no longer as present in our midst as it once was. The Vietnam War has shown us what misdeeds we are capable of even with the best of intentions. It has shown not only to us but to other peoples as well that we are not fundamentally different from other nations, that we are heir to the same kind of evil, to the same kind of sins the human flesh in general is heir to. This destruction, or at least this drastic weakening, of the peculiarity of American life, of American existence, of American values has had a disastrous effect upon our domestic life, upon the image of ourselves in our own eyes, and it has had a similarly disastrous effect upon the judgment which other nations have developed of us. I am always impressed, when I talk to foreign scholars and intellectuals, by the extent to which they are aware of what we have done to ourselves by engaging in the excesses of Vietnam and by our incapability thus far of stopping them. Thus when all is said and done about American foreign policy, we ought not to lose sight of that ultimate source of strength which is not in foreign policy itself but in the quality of our national existence.